MW01519545

FOCUS
ON THEM

Leading the **Mindset Revolution** for
Coaches, Educators, and Business Leaders

Dave Gosselin, PhD

Print ISBN: 978-1-61206-115-3
eBook ISBN: 978-1-61206-114-6

Interior and Cover Design by: Fusion Creative Works, www.fusioncw.com
Lead Editor: Jennifer Regner

For more information, visit www.DaveGosselinPhD.com

Published by

AlohaPublishing.com

First Printing
Printed in the United States of America

DEDICATION

This book is dedicated to my two daughters: Amy, who got me involved in coaching, and Megan, who challenged me to become better; and to my wife, Beth, for her patience and continuing support along my leadership journey.

CONTENTS

FIGURES

TABLES

A leader is best when people barely know he exists, when his work is done, his aim fulfilled, they will say: we did it ourselves.

— Lao Tzu, Chinese Philosopher

INTRODUCTION

Leadership is the art of getting someone else to do something
you want done because he wants to do it.

— Dwight D. Eisenhower

Over the past thirty years, I have had what I feel is a unique developmental journey. My journey has included the opportunity to be an effective educator and academic leader at the collegiate level, working as part of interdisciplinary teams, and also to provide community-oriented service and outreach. I have had the distinct pleasure of working collaboratively with faculty, administrators, students, farmers and ranchers, K-12 educators, and local, state, and federal government agencies.

As the result of what seemed like a simple question from my daughter, who was eight years old at the time, "Will you coach my soccer team?" I developed a passion for coaching young people. This, in turn, provided me the pathway to training coaching colleagues, helping them improve their skills, and learning from them along the way.

Most recently, I have invested time learning about and applying business-related assessment tools used to help develop leadership and collaboration skills among educational colleagues, players, and students so they can be more effective on the field, in the classroom, or in the workforce. I certainly do not claim to be a business expert, but it is clear to me the needs for business leaders are very similar, if not identical, to those in education and coaching.

I have been humbled by the recognition for my efforts by receiving: the 2014 Omtvedt Innovation Award for Science Education at the University of Nebraska–Lincoln; a nomination as finalist for the 2013 Floyd S. Oldt Boss of the Year by the University of Nebraska Office Professionals Association; the 2013 Nebraska High School Coach of the Year Small Parochial School, and 2009 Regional Coach of the Year from the National Soccer Coaches Association of America; a Lifetime Achievement Award in 2007 from the Nebraska State Soccer Association; Volunteer of the Year in 2005 from the Youth Sports Branch, YMCA, Lincoln, NE; and the 1999 Catalyst Award from the Nebraska Association of Teachers of Science.

On my journey, I have been influenced by many things, including interactions with a wide range of leadership styles—some good, and some downright bad. Just as you have, I have experienced different leadership models and philosophies as a student, a player, a coach, an educator, and as a member of various organizations, big and small. Most recently, through interactions with new colleagues developed through Talent Training International, it has become clear that coaches, educators, and business leaders struggle with the same leadership challenges.

At one point, I saw leadership as a complex and perplexing activity. However, as I reflect on my leadership journey so far, being a leader has definitely been a challenge, but I think, in general, we may make it more challenging than it needs to be.

As I have reflected back on my experiences, explored many resources—journal articles, books, webpages, etc., attended workshops, and conversed with people who coach and help develop business leaders, it has become increasingly clear to me that for any of us to maximize our effectiveness as a coach, educator, or leader in business, we need a mindset change that focuses on the needs of those we lead. We must keep reminding ourselves that it is not about you, the leader. Leading is about building relationships with those who look up to you. It's about building relationships between the people and what they do, and recognizing our capacity to influence others at a variety of levels. As pointed out by John C. Maxwell, a nationally recognized author on leadership, "Leadership is not about titles, positions or flowcharts. It is about one life influencing another." Changing our focus away from ourselves and towards others simplifies the challenge of leadership. We need to focus on them.

It was Drew Dudley's 2010 TEDx talk in Toronto[1] that introduced me to the concept of the "lollipop moment" and highlighted the capacity that every person has to influence someone else's life, to be a leader. We have all experienced a "lollipop" where someone said something or did something that fundamentally made our life better. Dudley tells a story about his "lollipop moment" and goes on to say that "every single one of you has been the catalyst for a lollipop moment. You have made someone's life better by something that you said or that you did . . . it is so scary to think of ourselves as that powerful. It can be frightening to think that we can matter that much to other people, because as long as we make leadership something bigger than us, as long as we keep leadership something beyond us, as long as we make it about changing the world, we give ourselves an excuse not to expect it every day from ourselves and from each other."

The essence of the "lollipop moment" is that we all have the ability to influence others, to be a leader in some way, shape, or form, and can have a huge impact on others if we change our focus from ourselves to others.

CHAPTER 1

Change Your Focus

We can all learn to lead.

— Simon Sinek, *Start with Why:*
How Great Leaders Inspire Everyone to Take Action

Every day we see evidence around us that we need more effective leadership. Daily, we read in the newspaper about gridlock in Washington, D.C., and to varying degrees at state and local government levels. As the Eisenhower quote at the beginning of the book illustrates, leadership requires a change of focus to the people you want to work with to get something done. Based on the current atmosphere in Washington, D.C., one may question whether this type of focus exists among our political leaders.

In our professional lives, we have all experienced those in leadership positions who claim they want input from different perspectives, but don't have an effective mechanism to get the input they desire. In addition, we have all put our faith in leaders who have not followed through on what they said they would do. We have all experienced leaders who claim to have all the answers. Unfortunately, they do not have the right questions, because they have not effectively engaged with those who could help them identify and/or clarify the questions.

During our educational careers, especially in higher education, we have all experienced the one-size-fits-all approach to learning. One of the primary drivers of this is the age-old assumption that if the instructor learned this way, then it must work for everyone. The focus was on the instructor and not on the students.

We have all experienced some of the craziness of youth sports, which manifests itself in many ways. Many people make their living coaching and training youth players, as the importance of club sports has expanded. Although they claim that the focus is on the success of the youth player, the actions of some coaches in these venues are not consistent with this claim and are more consistent with a focus on their personal success, measured by numbers of championships won and NCAA Division I players produced.

At the game level, we have all seen coaches getting more than a little carried away, blaming referees or yelling at players. Or in my case, it was taking many days to get over my eight-year-old daughter's recreational soccer team losing a game. I took these losses, early in my coaching career, quite personally and as a negative reflection on me. It took me quite some time to realize that, 30 seconds after the game was over, these third grade girls had moved on with their lives. To them the game was about playing and having fun. I wish I could say I've completely overcome my tendency to take the loss personally, but I have reduced the time it affects me from 168 hours down to less than 24. The outcomes of those games were not about me.

Over the years, many leadership models have been developed to describe the process or framework for learning, applying, and adapting leadership for given groups, organizations, or situations. We have all experienced different leadership philosophies, or ways of thinking and behaving as a leader. A leader's philosophy is driven by the individual's values and beliefs and is reflected in a person's leadership style. We experience this style by the way the leader behaves towards others. This behavior is strongly influenced by the leader's personality and leadership goals, and by the perceived relationship they want between themselves as leaders, and their so-called followers. We have all experienced what we recognize as good leaders, as well as those who really left something to be desired.

I would be willing to bet that when you reflect back on those leaders you saw as the good ones, to some extent you felt their focus was more on you than it was on them. When I reflect back to my days as a graduate student, I remember how my Ph.D. advisor, Dr. Jim Papike, treated us. We were treated with respect as scientists-in-training. We were given voice at meetings and in the operational aspects of the research group. We were well supported by the professional staff and involved in many social and professional activities. This respectful approach and focus on our professional development had a huge influence on me and the way in which I work with students and professional staff.

We all have different criteria for judging the quality of leadership that we have experienced. These criteria are based on our past experiences and what we have been led to believe is good leadership.

Throughout my leadership journey, I have increasingly spent time reflecting on the leadership landscape, the experiences I have had with a range of leaders, and my own trials and tribulations as a leader, teacher, and coach. These reflections have led me to the conclusion that to change the leadership landscape, it cannot be about us, as leaders. It needs to be about who we lead, teach, and coach. It needs to be about them! This change of focus helps reduce the complexity of leadership.

TAKING SOMEONE TO A NEW PLACE

As a society, we have a tendency to compartmentalize things. We often consider coaching, teaching, and leading as separate activities. However, a quick website search on coaching versus teaching, teaching versus leading, leading versus coaching, etc., indicates that these three activities have many common attributes. Overall, at their most basic level, all three are about taking someone to a new place (Figure 1).

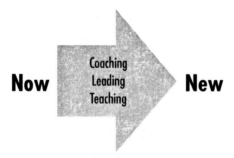

Figure 1. Coaching, leading, and teaching have the common goal of taking a person from where they are now to someplace new. These three terms will be used interchangeably throughout the book.

When an individual takes a journey to someplace new, change is involved. To change, people need to learn. Helping others learn is about helping people engage their brains in what they are doing.

Therefore, using an approach that integrates the best practices for helping people learn should improve one's ability to lead, coach, and teach (i.e., to influence their development). I refer to this as educating, coaching, and leading with the brain in mind. The beauty of using a brain-based approach to leading, coaching, and teaching is that we embrace the viewpoint that all three of these activities, at their most fundamental level, are about helping people learn. All three activities—educating, coaching, and leading—involve people learning a new subject, how to play a team sport, or how to fit into a company culture and do a job.

The most effective learning environments occur with an engaged community[2] and where a collaborative environment exists. Creating a collaborative environment is not as easy as it sounds. In the late 1990s, I learned some important lessons about collaboration as part of a research project I was leading that brought scientists, classroom teachers, and students preparing to be teachers together to work on a common project. As we examined the effectiveness of the teams, it was clear that several of the teams formed working relationships very quickly and as a result, identified tasks to be accomplished, divided responsibilities, and worked like fine-tuned machines.

However, several of the teams were on the opposite end of the effectiveness spectrum. In fact, based on reading their daily journals, if they had weapons, the situation could have become downright ugly at times. This led us to several questions. Why were some of our research teams far more productive than others? Why did these teams accomplish much more than the others? What can we do in the future to build more effective research teams?

In addition to the learning going on at the individual level, the more productive teams formed strong relationships among the individuals as they were taking their journey to someplace new. In other words, the more productive teams possessed collaborative qualities that were lacking in the less effective groups. These qualities emerged because the team members invested time in developing their relationships with each other. The people in these groups developed and shared a common vision for their project. They treated each other as equals and they valued each other's contributions. They were intrinsically motivated. They shared responsibility and accountability for the outcomes of the project as well. They effectively worked together to get to someplace new. More on this later.

FROM THE NOW TO THE NEW: CHANGE YOUR MINDSET

If we invoke the K.I.S.S—Keep It Simple Stupid—principle, a simple mindset change at two levels—individual and organizational—can make a huge difference in our effectiveness as leaders, coaches, and educators. These levels are illustrated in Figure 2. The first and most fundamental mindset change begins with the recognition that leading is not about you. It is about your ability to create an environment to maximize the abilities of those whom you are leading and their potential to be successful. It is about taking each person to someplace new by enhancing the learning environment through a brain-based approach (Figure 2, above the arrow). This mindset shift recognizes that every person on "your team" brings something unique to the group. It is up to you as the "leader" to help them maximize their contributions on their way to someplace new.

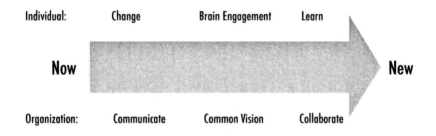

Figure 2. A mindset shift to effectively move individuals and organizations from where they are now to someplace new requires change and learning at the personal level, and employment of strategies that foster communication and collaboration among groups of people.

The second level of the mindset shift focuses on the organization (Figure 2, below the arrow). At this level, the emphasis is on communication to create a common vision, which is a critical element for collaboration. This collaboration-based approach creates an environment to maximize the abilities of each team member.

The more I practice leadership, think about leadership, read about leadership, and hear people talk about leaders they admire, the clearer it becomes. Changing your mindset to focus on taking individuals and your organization from the "now" to the "new" (Figure 2) will improve your effectiveness as a leader.

To help facilitate this shift in mindset for you as a leader, it is important for you to:

- Know yourself;

- Know the learning, behavioral, and motivational styles, among others, of those you lead;

- Use methods that are developmentally appropriate for your students, players, and employees to facilitate and maximize learning;

- Employ methods to articulate where it is you want your team, class, or organization to go, and develop a plan to get there;

- Develop a culture that continuously assesses and reflects, individually and collectively, on what works, what did not work, and what needs to be improved;

- Learn methods that facilitate communication and a collaborative culture where questions are expected.

The purpose of this book is to help you as a leader bring together these components using five questions and the key components of learning, collaboration, and communication, while avoiding assumptions that can take you down some slippery slopes (see Figure 3).

At face value, the five questions appear to be relatively simple. In reality, they are potentially very challenging questions for you to ask yourself (see Figure 3):

- Who am I as a leader?

- Whom am I leading?

- Where do I want to lead them?

- How do I get them there?

- How do we know when we get there?

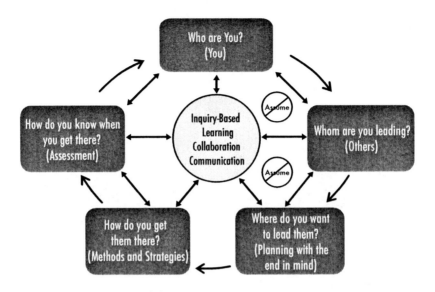

Figure 3. The five basic questions.

In addition to these questions, the following propositions provide a basic framework for the approach presented.

1. As a teacher, coach, or employer, your goal is to take those who are under your mentorship someplace new.

2. To take them someplace new requires change, and learning is a prerequisite to change.

3. The methods and strategies embedded in these activities need to engage the brain to maximize learning.

4. A collaborative approach to these activities will make teaching, coaching, and leading more effective.

5. A collaborative approach requires, at the very minimum, the creation of a common vision among your team.

6. To create a common vision among the different people requires a range of approaches; this requires knowledge of who you are as a leader and whom you are leading, and a com-

mitment to minimizing assumptions about those you are leading.

7. People are different, yet they are all valuable and can contribute uniquely to the team if given the opportunity.

8. An environment for effective communication is foundational to success.

As you read this book and apply the approach using the five questions and the framework propositions, I would like to hear from you about how the approach has increased your effectiveness as a leader, coach, or teacher. In the long term, I am confident it will help you, your team, and your organization be more successful. Please share your stories on my website, DaveGosselinPhD.com.

CHAPTER 2

Who Are You and Why Does It Matter?

If you want to change others, you first must change yourself.

— Judy Suiter, Founder and President, Competitive Edge, Inc.

The basic premise of this book is that our leadership journey should focus on those we are trying to take to someplace new—how we are going to get them there, and how we will know when we get there. However, to help others move forward, it is important to understand ourselves. Although I had been exposed to this concept through a variety of leadership courses early in my professional career, it only became obvious to me as a result of my relationships with two colleagues who I would call my education and coaching mentors, Dr. Ron Bonnstetter and Dr. Doug Williamson, respectively.

UNDERSTANDING SELF

In one of the first courses of my soccer coaching career, Doug, who is a senior staff instructor for the National Soccer Association of America, emphasized the importance of articulating your coaching philosophy. This required me to look into myself and figure out what I truly value and believe about coaching. If you do not know that about yourself, how can you articulate it to your players and parents? In addition, Doug exposed me to Gallup's Seven Demands of Leaders (http://www.gallup.com/businessjournal/11614/seven-demands-leadership.aspx). One of these demands is knowing self. In the Gallup literature, it has been well documented that effective leaders know their strengths and weaknesses and don't assume that they know everything.[3] Knowing yourself requires reflection and thinking about these types of things.

Through my work with Ron, I was introduced to the process of reflection about self and how it can be aided by the use of a wide range of assessment instruments that can provide information about your behavioral and motivational characteristics, among other attributes (more on this below). Through Ron, I met a new colleague, Andy Johnson, who lives his life in the business world. In his book *Pushing Back Entropy*,[4] Andy emphasizes the importance of knowing self. He indicates that differences between people can be placed into three categories: the things we didn't choose, things that we choose, and things that are the mixture of the two. Johnson eloquently describes the things we didn't choose as the hand we're dealt. These include things that are controlled by natural processes, and those related to nurturing or the environment we grew up in, that at the time we had no control over. Natural factors include such things as age, gender, race, physical traits, and types of intelligences a la Howard Gardner, as outlined in his book *Frames of Mind*.[5] Nurturing factors include socioeconomic status, family of origin, religious background, and early childhood experiences, among others. We also have the ability to choose our own destiny to some extent and within certain limitations.

Some examples of these types of choices include how we view ourselves, how we choose to view others, the extent to which we want to learn, our ethical perspectives regarding right and wrong, and our abilities to manage our emotions. Johnson also refers to what he calls "a mixed bag" of characteristics that are a mixture of nature, nurture, and choice. The mixed bag includes behavioral style, the motivators that drive our behaviors, attachment style, and introversion/extroversion.

It very important to recognize that we all have our own tendencies related to how we interact with other people. Some interpret these tendencies or behavioral styles as good or bad, when in reality they are just different. Behavioral styles are influenced by many things. Regardless of the origin of your behavioral style, it is important for you to understand your own patterns and tendencies because they will influence how you interact with other people, how you communicate with them, and how they perceive you. Johnson puts it best when he states that, "Healthy teams work to understand their own styles and the styles of the others on the team, so they can communicate and work with others."

HOW WE ACT: OUR BEHAVIOR

One tool that I have found very useful in characterizing my own pattern of behavior is the behavior assessment tool DISC.[6] It is part of Talent Training International's TriMetrix® Assessment (Figure 4).

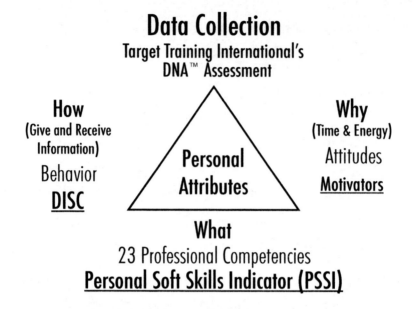

Figure 4. The TriMetrix® DNA™ Assessment provides information about the behaviors, motivators, and professional competencies for individuals.

The DISC assessment describes a person's behavioral style on a continuum of four primary behavioral dimensions that results in 384 distinct patterns. These dimensions are:

- D dimension: how an individual manages problems/challenges.

- I dimension: how a person uses their influence with people.

- S dimension: in the simplest terms, their steadiness, which reflects how the person deals with pace and change.

- C dimension: how an individual deals with procedures and complying with rules and other constraints that may be placed on them by an organization.

Important: Our behavior is a blend of all four dimensions that results in everyone having their own DISC profile.

Over the years, understanding the differences in my behavioral style has played an important role in my work with Ron Bonnstetter. Our DISC profiles are shown in Figure 5. In the language of DISC, which is referred to as the universal language of observable human behavior, I am described as having a high C, low D style. The dominant traits of the high C style include being detailed oriented, meticulous, orderly, diplomatic, accurate, precise, and some might say a perfectionist. For the low D part of my style, some of the words that can be used to describe me include low-keyed, cautious, unsure, hesitant, agreeable, modest, and peaceful. In contrast, Ron, one of my closest colleagues and friends, has a high D, low C style. The dominant traits of the high D include competitive, strong-willed, short-tempered, determined, and aggressive. The low C style yields the following traits: nonconforming, individualistic, careless, independent, creative, uninhibited, and unsystematic. A quick comparison of the traits for our inherent styles would suggest that we are opposites in the ways we approach the world. In the beginning of our relationship, I could not understand why he had such challenges putting together text for a proposal in the correct format or assembling a budget for a grant. I could also not understand why he always waited until the last minute to complete a task, whereas I had completed the task days, if not weeks, before the deadline.

After years of working together, the differences between the two of us became very clear to me when we had the opportunity to compare our DISC profiles. Our DISC assessments supported what we had been doing for years, that is, we were adapting to each for success. It was nice to get this confirmation; however, it would have

been better to have known years before so we could have reduced
the amount of energy that we had to put in to making our partnership work. Knowledge of our DISC would have been powerful.

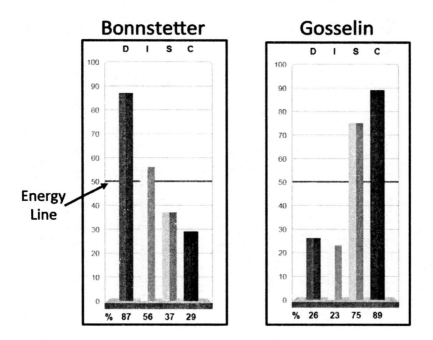

Figure 5. DISC profiles for Ron Bonnstetter and Dave Gosselin. These
patterns illustrate the influence of each DISC dimension relative to the energy
line. Your core style is the highest point above the energy line, which is located
at 50% on a 100-point scale. The energy line indicates how strong an individual's preference for that style is. No core style is better than another. This
line is used to determine the key characteristics of a person's profile. Used with
permission from the authors and publisher, Target Training International.

Our behavioral differences illustrate the value of diversity in teams
and how differences can be strengths, when one understands what
each member brings to the table. As we have grown as a team, we
have come to focus on our strengths. A crucial takeaway message is
that effective leaders need to see the potential contribution of those

team members that are in fact the opposites of themselves. As leaders we also need to embrace what each of us is NOT and see that in another person—someone who is an opposite, and has qualities that may be missing from oneself. For example, words that can be used to describe me include low-keyed, cautious, unsure, hesitant, agreeable, modest, and peaceful—and those that are used to describe Ron include competitive, strong-willed, short-tempered, determined, and aggressive. At times, we have found that it is good to have these differences in our characteristics. Appreciating our diversity and, at the same time, recognizing the balance it has brought to our team has been important to our collaboration.

Recognizing what we are not and what someone else is does not represent a weakness in the other person, but a difference that may be essential to the success of a team. Differences are neither good nor bad; they are just different and can strengthen a team.

WHY WE ACT THE WAY WE DO

In contrast to our behaviors that are quite visible, the drivers for what we do are often hidden, and not readily observable or easily articulated. These hidden motivators are the "whys" behind what we do. They include our personal values and our passions. Our motivators are the values and beliefs we have developed over time. They are integral parts of us; some we may be born with and others are the result of our interactions with the outside world. The choices that we make to invest time, energy, resources, and money are indicators of our hidden motivations. As Simon Sinek highlights in his book *Start with Why: How Great Leaders Inspire Everyone to Take Action*,[7] our choices and decisions are made in the limbic brain which is powerful, and where the "why" for the "what" and "how" of our actions lie. Motivators are like an engine beneath the hood of a car. It isn't really seen by the outside world, but it is what powers us and fuels our behaviors. We need to know our "whys" and those of others.

Fundamental to effective interaction with others is knowledge about the motivators that drive us as individuals. These motivators initiate behavior and are sometimes called the hidden motivators because they are not readily observed. One tool that I have used to help characterize hidden motivators is the assessment developed by Target Training International based on Spranger (1928).[8] Figure 6 is my motivational profile in the context of the six primary motivators that includes the following drivers:

- **Theoretical** – People who have this driver want to know and discover. They have a passion for learning. They love to study, read, take classes, and conduct research. When they get involved with something new, they want to learn as much as they can. They want knowledge for knowledge's sake. They will appear to be intellectual and have a tendency to be cognitive, empirical, critical, and rational.

- **Individualistic** – Individuals who have this driver, which is sometimes called the political motivator, have a desire for power, control, and recognition. They have a desire to control their own destiny and that of others as well. In some people with certain personalities, this motivator is expressed by a desire for personal power, influence, and renown. They like to lead and advance their position.

- **Social** – People who have this driver, which is also referred to as the social worker or altruistic motivator, value people and are kind, sympathetic, and unselfish. Helping others is high on their list of things to do. They are selfless and have a desire to give back to the community, give to charities, solve global social problems, etc. They are typically generous with their time, talents, and resources.

- **Utilitarian** – Individuals who have this driver have a desire to get a positive return on investment, which may be in the form of time, energy, or financial. They have a characteristic interest in money, accumulation of wealth, and what is useful. They will focus on practical results. They seek money for the security of their present and future family, not necessarily just for themselves. Sometimes this motivator drives people to want to have more than others.

- **Aesthetic** – People who have this driver have a strong desire to create harmonious outcomes. They may perceive life as a procession of events, each that needs to be enjoyed for its own sake. Life is about experience and they have a tendency to be sensitive about conflict. They have an inherent interest in form, beauty, and harmony in the work. They will enjoy various forms and functions of art. Long range planning is a strength because they have a desire to create harmonious outcomes.

- **Traditional** – Individuals who have this as a strong driver have a desire to live by a certain set of standards and/or beliefs upon which they base decisions. They adhere to defined rules, regulations, and principles for living. Commonly, they have very strong faith and/or cultural values. Their traditional values may stem from a variety of sources based on family and culture. They may or may not embrace a religion.

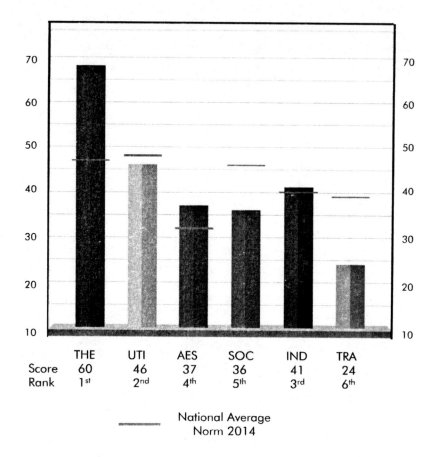

	THE	UTI	AES	SOC	IND	TRA
Score	60	46	37	36	41	24
Rank	1st	2nd	4th	5th	3rd	6th

———— National Average
Norm 2014

Figure 6. Motivation profile for the author. Used with permission from the author and publisher, Target Training International.

As you can see in Figure 6, my primary driver is the theoretical motivator that pushes me towards the desire to acquire knowledge and be empirical, critical, and rational. I prefer facts to feelings and have a tendency to question things. I show very little emotion and try to be as objective as possible. Many of my students have the aesthetic driver as their primary motivator. To the aesthetics, I may seem to be a closed-minded know-it-all, while I have difficulty with their tendency to be subjective and go with their feelings instead of the facts. Knowing about these differences has helped me improve my interactions with the students, at least from my perspective.

There are other attributes that can be measured and a variety of instruments can be used. Regardless of the approach, knowing yourself is important. The value of "self-awareness" as a critical trait for successful leaders was emphasized in a study of more than 72 executives at public and private companies with revenues from $50 million to $5 billion. This study,[9] conducted in 2010 by Green Peak Partners and Cornell's School of Industrial and Labor Relations, examined interpersonal traits, but the finding that most resonated with me was this one:

> Leadership searches give short shrift to 'self-awareness,' which should actually be a top criterion. Interestingly, a high self-aware-ness score was the strongest predictor of overall success. This is not altogether surprising as executives who are aware of their weaknesses are often better able to hire subordinates who per-form well in categories in which the leader lacks acumen. These leaders are also more able to entertain the idea that someone on their team may have an idea that is even better than their own.

One last thought on the importance of self-awareness from the late Warren Bennis, who was a professor at the University of Southern California and recognized expert on leadership, said the following in his seminal book *On Becoming A Leader:*[10]

> To become a leader, then, you must become yourself, become the maker of your own life. . . . 'Know thyself,' was the in-scription over the Oracle at Delphi. And it is still the most difficult task that any of us faces. But until you truly know

yourself, strengths and weaknesses, know what you want to do and why you want to do it, you cannot succeed in any but the most superficial sense of the word.

Suffice it to say, developing self-awareness not only benefits you as a leader in identifying your own strengths, but it also benefits those with whom you are taking your leadership journey, and opens the door to the recognition that there is more to learn. We do not develop self-awareness in just "one season" . . . it takes years, it takes practice, and realistically should never end. As leaders, coaches, and teachers, we expect those that we lead to learn new skills and practice. We should expect no less of ourselves when it comes to reflecting on and learning self-awareness to improve the organization.

CHAPTER 3

Who Are You and What Are Your Philosophies, Values, and Ethics?

The greatest leader is not necessarily the one who does the greatest things. He is the one that gets the people to do the greatest things.

— Ronald Reagan

Although you may have never articulated it, you have a coaching philosophy. Everybody does. You have a set of values and beliefs regarding how someone should coach, what they should be coaching, etc. And, just as everyone has a coaching philosophy, everybody has a leadership philosophy and style. Your approach will vary from autocratic to participatory. Everybody also has a working model for how people should be taught and how they learn.

IDENTIFYING YOUR PHILOSOPHIES, STYLES, AND MODELS

Before attempting to lead, coach, or educate, it is extremely important for you to reflect on your philosophies, styles, and models. And you must articulate what you believe and value to those you are coaching, teaching, and leading. By reflecting and articulating, you are modeling the behavior you want your students, players, and employees to have.

One of the first things I do when teaching a coaching course is ask the participants to think about their coaching philosophy in the context of the hows and whys of everything they do as a coach. Your philosophy—your beliefs, your values—guides all of your actions, on and off the field. I provide them with time to write the answers to the following questions:

- Why do you coach?
- What are your goals for your players?
- What experiences do you want to offer your players?
- How do you define success?
- What do you believe and value about sports?

A very similar set of questions can be used in educational and business environments.

The answers to these questions describe your beliefs and values regarding coaching. And, they provide the rules of conduct that guide your coaching—also referred to as your ethics. For soccer coaches, the National Soccer Coaches Association of America has established a code of ethics for coaches. From a professional perspective, the rules of conduct that you live or work by may be a set of ethics developed by a professional organization. The Association of American Educators has developed a code of ethics for educators. It is important to use these guides as you develop and articulate the principles that will guide your actions.

SHARING YOUR VALUES & BELIEFS

Reflecting on your values and beliefs, especially in the context of your hidden motivators, will lead to self-awareness, self-disclosure, and self-confidence. And, sharing your values leads to trust. Players, students, and employees want to follow leaders/coaches/teachers they feel they can trust and know where they stand. The importance of trust will be addressed later in the book.

Over the years, I have articulated the following philosophical elements as a soccer coach.

1. I coach because I want to help players become better players, and provide them with opportunities to practice life skills that will help them succeed in the world beyond the soccer field.

2. My primary goal is to have a team that has fun playing soccer. If our players do not have fun playing, why should they play? Soccer is not a job. It's not homework. It's supposed to be fun.

3. I want to create experiences so that each individual can make the choice to give their best during practices and games as well as to play with pride, determination, and heart. I want players to improve each training session and over the entire season.

4. Our goal is to win and be as competitive as we can during each game. However, our overall success will be measured on player and team improvement. Under all circumstances, we will win or lose with class.

5. I want our players to learn to think on their own while playing. To do this, they must be willing to try new things and make mistakes. We want our players to know that it is okay to make mistakes. The only way to never make a mistake is to never try and do anything new. We want each player to learn

lots of things, so that means they will make mistakes. We'll actually play better if they try to do new things.

I strongly encourage parents to ask the coach of any team on which their son or daughter plays what their philosophy is.

Successful coaches/leaders will not necessarily have identical philosophies; however, they need to have a philosophy and need to be clear about that philosophy with those they lead. A little side note—in numerous publications related to selecting a club sport coach, or deciding where one will play their selected sport in college, it is emphasized that if one does not see the words fun or enjoyment of the game in their coaching philosophy, one should be very careful.

My leadership philosophy is very strongly linked to collaboration. It has not always been that way. Changes in my overall leadership philosophy interestingly track very well with observations and analysis of traditional coaching to modern coaching made by accomplished sports psychologist Bill Beswick, in his 2001 book, *Focused for Soccer*.[11]

From grade school to high school into college, my view of leadership was very consistent with the traditional characteristics identified in Table 1, especially those italicized. I went to a high school in which everyone was required to participate in the junior ROTC. The word leader invoked images of George C. Scott as Patton, standing on a stage giving his final farewell—authoritarian and autocratic—very much about the results and inward focus. Some would describe it as being highly narcissistic. I considered leaders very special people. Only people with special characteristics could be leaders.

Fortunately, my leadership philosophy has evolved. It is much more in tune with the characteristics of what Beswick refers to as a *modern coach*—a person that is about "we," who is a teacher, an educator, and player-centered.[12] This transition has been influenced by many people, good and bad experiences, and by my strongest motivator, which is the theoretical driver and my interest in wanting to be a more effective leader. As a result of this internal motivator, when I get involved with something new, I want to learn as much as I can—so I have taken the time to study, read, take classes, and conduct research on leadership. Through this exploration I have reflected a lot on my past and present leadership approaches.

Table 1. Comparison of "traditional" versus "modern" coaches.

Traditional	Modern
Authoritarian	Democratic
Yells	Sells
Speaks	Listens, then speaks
Trainer	Teacher/educator
Ex-player	Qualified coach
Hard worker	Smart worker
Focused on winning	Focused on winning
Task-centered	Player-centered
Results-dominated	Excellence-dominated
Instinctive	Careful planning
Player-dependent	Coach-influenced
Isolated	Mentored
"Me"	"We"

Putting on my educator hat, during the first couple weeks of class I share my educational philosophy with my students. I call this section of the course, "Why I do the things I do." I start by addressing the fundamental question of why do I teach? My reasons for teaching and my primary goal are very much interrelated. My primary goal for students is for them to be successful in the class. For some, and perhaps most, success measurement is based on the final outcome, which for most is an A grade. For others, success is focused on the process and the extent to which they have improved various skill sets. For me, their success—which is hard to measure—is the extent to which they develop an urge to learn more for the sake of knowing more. In essence, helping them develop a growth mindset so they become continuous and life-long learners.

In the context of what do I believe and value, my basic premise for this part of the course is that we teach the way we believe people learn. As will be outlined more explicitly later in the book, knowledge is constructed and, in this context, my goal is to use strategies that will help students build their knowledge and understanding. As a foundation for this aspect of the course, I introduce students to what I refer to as the brain-based, conceptual approach for how people learn. First and foremost, I emphasize that the process of learning physically changes the brain. In order to maximize the physical changes and therefore the learning, the content and information that we receive through our senses in the back cortex of the brain must be used by the parts of the brain in the frontal cortex. This transformation results in long-term learning, which is demonstrated by applying knowledge and skills in new situations. I want students to know why I do the things we do in class. I return to these reasons throughout the class. I also want them to reflect on how they think they learn. This part of the class also communicates to them that I value and am enthusiastic about teaching. An underlying goal of this approach is to increase their trust level.

ENGAGING INTELLECTUALLY

In my efforts to take my students, players, and employees to someplace new, I want them to have experiences that engage them intellectually with what they are doing. My philosophy is that I want them to ask their questions. At its most fundamental level, engagement starts with questions and inquiry. Questions and inquiry engage the brain at many levels and should drive the learning process. Questions range from relatively simple clarifying questions, which require minimal intellectual engagement, to complex probing questions, which require significant intellectual engagement. Clarifying questions are simple questions of fact. They have brief, factual answers that promote low-order thinking. Developing and asking probing questions requires thinking at a deeper level. An important test for a clarifying question is how long it takes to think about the question. For example, if a person has to pause and take time to ponder a question that has been asked, it was almost certainly a probing question. Probing questions require more time to address because they promote complex, higher-order thinking. This level of thinking is required for a person to become a problem solver, whether it is in the classroom, on the field, or in the business arena.

Volumes have been written about the importance of questions in engaging people in the learning process. On a daily basis, I try to practice the skill of questioning. It is not easy because we have not been conditioned to ask questions. For more on this, watch Sir Ken Robinson's TED talks from 2006 and 2010 (2006: http://www.ted.com/talks/ken_robinson_says_schools_ kill_creativity?language=en; 2010: http://www.ted.com/talks/ sir_ken_robinson_bring_on_the_revolution?language=en).

When I use questions, my goal is to engage the person in the learning process that will enhance their abilities to master the task at hand, increase conceptual understanding, and promote both simple (low-order) and complex (high-order) thinking.

Another important experience that helps people engage intellectually is the creation of a collaborative environment. Learning is a social endeavor, and creating community amongst learners only enhances the process. A collaborative environment in which questions are encouraged provides the opportunity for the development of shared goals and solutions to problems, for the exchange of information, and to share their personal expertise. All of these things together enhance trust.

CONSIDER YOUR IMPACT

Your process of reflection and articulation will likely be very different than mine, but another important thing to keep in mind is the potential impact that you have on those you lead. These impacts can be positive or negative, depending on many factors. If you think back about a teacher, coach, or boss who had a major impact on you, I suspect one of your key memories is how they cared about you. One person who had a huge impact on my life was my homeroom teacher and high school instructor, Robert C. His impact on me was huge. It was not what he said—it was how he acted, it was how he respected me enough to listen, it was how he let me be heard, and it was how he challenged me to think about things differently. At the time, I did not see him as a leader, but, in fact, he was. He influenced me tremendously and certainly helped take me to someplace new.

SHOW THEM YOU CARE

As you consider your philosophies, consider the effectiveness of your abilities to take people to someplace new; consider whether your actions make people feel that you care about them. Teddy Roosevelt said, "Nobody cares how much you know, until they know how much you care." For many professionals in business, coaching, and educating, especially those of the male persuasion, the concept of caring comes across as very touchy-feely. To some extent it is. However, when all is said and done, if your players/students/employees know you care about them, they will trust you. When people sense that you really care about them, their level of trust increases, and they will go with you on the journey to someplace new.

Developing trust is the foundation for successful teams and organizations.[13] If you think back to those people you consider to be the best coach, teacher, or manager you have had, I am fairly confident that you got the sense that they cared about you, which led you to trust them.

In a powerful 2011 TED talk entitled, "Listen, Learn, Then Lead" (http://www.ted.com/talks/stanley_mcchrystal?language), General Stanley McChrystal describes an "after action review" designed, in theory, to teach him what he had done wrong after his platoon produced a less than stellar performance in an early morning training operation. He was taken through the entire operation step-by-step, telling him everything he did wrong . . . "sort of leadership by humiliation. They put a big screen up, and they take you through everything—'and then you didn't do this, and you didn't do this, etc.'" When he left the briefing, he walked out feeling as "low as a snake's belly in a wagon rut" and was on his way to apologize to his battalion commander and admit that he had let him down. He went up to begin the apology and his commander said, "'Stanley, I thought you did great.' And in one sentence, he lifted me, put me back on my feet, and taught me that leaders can let you fail and yet not let you be a failure." Near the end of his talk, McChrystal goes further to say that as leaders " . . . you have to watch and take care of each other. I probably learned the most about relationships. I learned they are the sinew which holds the force together."

If you accept the premise that caring for those you lead is important, how is this articulated in your philosophy, through the type of experiences you want to provide and the actions you take that will show your players/students/employees that you care? From my own experiences, the actions you take may be what some might consider relatively simple things that you do for them or say to them. They will know you care if your actions match your words (i.e., your philosophy).

ACTIONS SPEAK LOUDER THAN WORDS

Actions do speak louder than words. Your actions need to be consistent with what you have stated your values and beliefs to be, otherwise you will slowly, but surely, lose credibility. They will know you care when you focus on how you listen to what they are saying and how you interact with them.

Do you listen authentically? That is, listen respectfully, respect their values and beliefs, and present genuine concern for their thoughts and ideas? Do you listen to them with empathy? The term "empathy" describes a wide range of experiences. The context used here is: empathy is the ability to sense the other person's emotions and to imagine what someone else might be thinking or feeling.

They will know you care when you provide constructive feedback that includes encouragement, identification of successes, as well as problems and challenges. Do you tell them when you see them do something well? Research by the University of Michigan Business School several years ago indicated that the frequency of praise versus criticism was reflected in team performance. In most cases the best-performing teams use positive comments much more often than negative ones. A ratio of six to one has been suggested. They will know you care when you do the little things you think they will never notice.

Whatever experiences you provide or actions you take, I hope you all have the opportunity to get a letter like the one I received from one of my players on my first club soccer team, the Star City Jazz, who I believe was seventeen years old at the time. It blew me away:

Dave,

Thank you so much for everything you have done for me and our whole team. I remember the first time I met you . . . your team needed some extra players for a tournament your team was going to be playing in, and I got asked to play. I was so excited to meet new people and have another coach teach me new moves.

So one day, (my coach) Rich decided we should scrimmage against you guys during one of our practices, and I was pumped and ready to play, trying to impress the guy I was going to be a guest player for. So when it was time for us to meet I thought to myself I better shake his hand because I knew that would leave a good impression. I walked up to you and stuck out my hand. You looked down at me and shook my hand and said, "Hi Anna, I am very excited to have you be a guest player on our team." Well, something like that.

I remember the first game I played with Jazz. I was excited and nervous at the same time. I remember scoring what I think was our only goal against the first team we played, and I also remember playing in goal and getting scored on too and being scared of Bailey because I was afraid I was not going to be good enough for the team.

I had a wonderful time playing for you. The one reason I joined the team was because of the coach you are to me and our whole team. I loved the speeches you gave us and how much confidence you would give me, before and after a game. You are a caring guy, probably the most generous and warm-hearted person I have met, always thinking about the team before yourself. You were always trying to do everything you could for our team. Sometimes I thought you were crazy because of all the things you would do for us. You would go and watch us play with our high school teams, and other sports we are in. You take the time to have goalie practices with me and Bailey, and plan practices for us to do. You plan games for us so we can get better and have more experience playing different teams at different levels. And lastly you take the time to write a letter to each person on the team and tell them what you think about them and what kind of person they are to you. I thought it would be right for you to get one too and that's why I am writing this to you.

I just want you to know how great a person you are to me, and what kind of impact you have had on my life, always wanting me to get better and try harder. Always asking how I am and (how) my other teammates are feeling. You are like a dad to us, wanting to know if anything is bothering us and wanting to help as much as you can.

Dave, thank you so much for everything, I will never forget you and I hope we stay in touch for years. Thanks again!

Love, Anna

CHAPTER 4

Understand Whom You Are Coaching/Leading/Educating

It is not easy in this world for one person to understand the next one.

— Johann Wolfgang von Goethe, 18th-century German statesman

WHOM ARE YOU LEADING? WHAT ARE THEIR CHARACTERISTICS? WHAT DO THEY BRING TO THE TABLE?

When working with a group of students, players, or employees, have you ever found yourself starting a sentence . . . When I was their age? When I was in school? When I got my first job? We did this, or we did that, or this or that worked for me, or we would have never done that. I know that I have done it. In fact, I still do it, but not as often. All of these statements reflect an inward-looking focus on you. I can hear you saying to yourself, he just spent the entire second chapter emphasizing the importance of knowing about ourselves and our tendencies. This was intentionally done because who you are is the foundation upon which all your relationships will be built. Relationships are at the heart of a team because that is how trust is built—without it you will have a dysfunctional team.[14]

Without doubt, it is a challenge to really know yourself and re-flect on yourself, because it can make you very uncomfortable. However, an even greater challenge is learning to know the people you are leading, which turns the focus from ourselves to them, in order to move to bigger and better things.

We need to constantly remind ourselves that educating, lead-ing, and coaching is not about you. It is about them, the audi-ence whom you are trying to help on their journey. As part of this journey to someplace new, you need to be consistently asking the question, who am I leading? The answer to that question is not trivial. To answer it requires investing time to learn about the char-acteristics of those you are leading. Some of these characteristics are easily observable—age, gender, height, weight, skill level, and behaviors to some extent. Other characteristics are not quite as ap-parent, including what motivates them, what are the details of their behavioral style, what are their mindsets, what are their values and beliefs, what do they know, what are their strengths, what are their weaknesses, what are they capable of doing, among many other questions. The extent to which any or all of these can be investigat-ed is dependent on the situation and the time available. The more you can invest in knowing your team, the better you can build off their strengths, and the more effective you will be.

BEHAVIORS AND MOTIVATORS

Several years ago, I was coaching a U-17 girls' premier-level soccer team and I received a very distressing phone call from a parent of one of my players. This parent indicated that the ongoing ac-tions of several of her daughter's teammates had created an envi-ronment on the team that was not the positive-type environment that I envisioned for my teams. Over the next couple of days I reflected on this call, observed teammate interactions, talked with Ron Bonnstetter, and consulted with my assistant coaches as well as some of the other players on the team. It became clear that there was not only a challenge that the team needed to address related to the behavioral problems, but an opportunity for me to learn more about my players and for them to learn more about themselves in the context of their behavioral characteristics and motivational drivers. This situation also provided the opportunity to apply the TTI assessments—DISC and Motivators—described in the previous chapter. The goal was to improve team collaboration, communication, and cohesion. To learn more about the talent assessments I use, contact me through my website at DaveGosselinPhD.com.

Behavioral Characteristics (DISC): The behavior data for the twenty players (circles) and two coaches (triangles) is presented on the TTI Success Insights Wheel® (Figure 7). The wheel is divided into four quadrants based on the influence that the four primary behavioral dimensions, D, I, S, and C, have on a person's overall behavioral characteristics. An analogy that can be used to help interpret the wheel is to imagine a magnet at D, I, S, and C. The stronger the dimension influences the behavior, the stronger the force the magnet has to pull away from the center of the circle. The wheel demonstrates the similarities and differences in behavioral characteristics among team members. It uses eight specific identifiers: conductor, persuader, promoter, relater, supporter, coordinator, analyzer, and implementor. The characteristics of each identifier are provided in the text adjacent to it. I am represented by two triangles, 7 and 8, because I took the assessment twice on different days to give a sense of the reproducibility of the results. Triangle 2 is the assistant coach. For more details regarding the interpretation of the wheels, see Bonnstetter and Suiter (2013).[15]

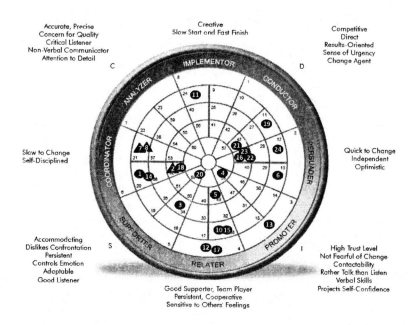

Figure 7. Behavior data for soccer players (circles) and coaches (triangles) presented on the TTI Success Insights Behavioral Team Wheel®. Used with permission from the author and publisher, Target Training International.

The assistant coach and I are coordinators whose strengths tend towards being self-disciplined; setting high standards of conduct and work; being alert to problems, rules, errors and procedures; having the ability to make tough decisions without letting emotions interfere; and emphasizing the need for quality. Fifteen percent of the players have similar characteristics. Thirty-five percent of the players are supporters and relaters who are very supportive of team activities. Relaters tend to: create an environment where people feel significant and support others in achieving goals; offer understanding and friendship; and show team loyalty. Supporters tend to: be understanding and good listeners; be patient and comforting; like to be in a team environment; and prefer an environment where long service is deemed important. Interestingly the three goal keepers (10, 12, 15), and a fourth (17) often willing to play keeper, when necessary, are relaters.

Motivational Characteristics: The top two motivational characteristics for the players and coaches are presented on a TTI Success Insights Motivational Team Wheel® (Figure 8). These data provide background on a person's motivators or fundamental drivers for their behavior. The six motivators that explain the "whys" behind a person's actions are: theoretical, utilitarian, aesthetic, social, individualistic, and traditional, as previously described. It is important to recognize that these motivators are not readily observed and are often hidden. Figure 8 highlights the primary and secondary motivators for the players and coaches because it is typically the top two motivators that drive behavior. This graph illustrates that 80% of the players are driven by social concerns. They thrive on: eliminating conflict and pain within the team; assisting with the needs and struggles of team members; and taking a personal interest in team members. Forty percent of the players are driven by theoretical factors through which these players thrive on: solving team problems, identifying and systematizing team activities, and pursuing knowledge and truth. Thirty percent of the players have individualistic factors that serve as secondary motivators. These factors include that they want to take a tactical approach to life and develop team relationships that advance their position within the team, whereby they can attain and use power. They want to lead the team while planning and carrying out a winning strategy.

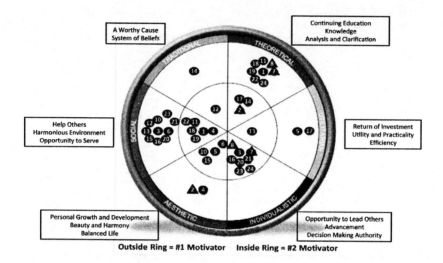

Outside Ring = #1 Motivator   Inside Ring = #2 Motivator

Figure 8. Behavior data for soccer players (circles) and coaches (triangles) presented on the TTI Success Insights Motivational Team Wheel. Used with permission from the author and publisher, Target Training International.

Application: There are many ways this information can be used to learn about the characteristics of your players. Prior to two practices early in the season, the team spent approximately 30 minutes in small groups of three to four using a TTI customized team report that included team wheels for behaviors and motivators (Figs. 7 and 8). Their team report also provided team-blending resources. An example is provided in Figure 9 that compares the behavioral tendencies of a persuader to a coordinator. A second example for motivational tendencies is given in Figure 10. I purposefully created the groups to include the players who were having the apparent problems with each other, #15 and #24. In the small groups, each player presented their behavioral and motivational characteristics. They discussed how these characteristics may influence how they interact with each other and how their behavioral tendencies may create roadblocks to effective communication both on and off the field.

Comparison of Behavioral Tendencies

Persuader ⟷ Coordinator

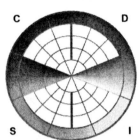

- Quick to Change to Slow to Change
- Enjoys Change to Avoids Change
- Extroverted to Introverted
- Animated to Reserved
- "We can do it" to "How do we do it?"
- Persuaders should spend time explaining project goals and expectations to the Coordinators.
- Persuaders should try to stick to the relevant facts.
- Coordinators will become frustrated with lack of instruction, follow up and follow through.
- Coordinators should make a conscious effort to be more direct and open with their feelings and concerns.

Figure 9. An example of a team-blending resource from TTI that compares the behavioral tendencies of people who are persuaders to coordinators. Used with permission from the author and publisher, Target Training International.

Comparison of Motivational Tendencies

Theoretical ⟷ Social

- Theoreticals will fail to see the logic in some of the high Social's choices when people get placed above the search for truth.
- Theoreticals will be accepting of a certain degree of pain or loss when seeking this truth, where the high Social will not be accepting of the same exchange.
- Fact driven choices can be insensitive to people and will be seen by Socials as a great injustice.
- Socials will not understand how the Theoreticals can reach such conclusions when the outcome is callous and uncaring.

Figure 10. An example of a team-blending resource from TTI that compares the motivational tendencies of people whose primary motivators are theoretical or social. Used with permission from the author and publisher, Target Training International.

As the coach who is a coordinator, it is important information for me to know who the persuaders are. They provide me with one of the biggest challenges because they need change, whereas I would prefer things not to change. Persuaders have a tendency to lack follow-through and this can create frustrations for me. Knowing that these characteristics exist amongst my players requires me to approach them differently than I would another player who is similar to me. Recognition of these differences by both parties allows each to adapt to the other's tendencies.

Going back to the original story, the challenges that were noted during the call to me were likely the result of differences in both behavioral tendencies (conductor/persuader #24, relative to relater/supporter #15) and motivational factors of players 15 and 24 (theoretical versus aesthetic). Table 2 illustrates some of the behavioral roadblocks that were likely contributing to the relationship challenges.

Table 2. Potential factors that may create conflicts between conductors and relaters/supporters/coordinators.

Conductor	Relater/Supporter/ Coordinator
Quick pace	Slow pace
Extroverted	Introverted
Impatient	Patient
Enjoys conflict	Avoids conflict
Quick to anger	Slow to anger
High risk	Low risk
Tendencies	
Conductors tend to overpower. They must work hard to build up a trusting relationship before relaters/supporters/coordinators feel comfortable verbalizing their concerns. Conductors need to be mindful of their listening skills as well as their diplomacy.	

Potential conflicts can also occur because of the influence of different motivators. The contrasts between the primary motivators of theoretical versus aesthetic also contributed to the relationship problems. To the aesthetic-dominated player, #15, the theoretically motivated player, #24, would appear to be a closed-minded know-it-all. In addition, the secondary motivator for #15 was social which leads to having issues with those motivated by individualistic tendencies, which was the second motivator for the theoretical-dominated player. At its most basic level, the socials will have issues with the individualistics' tendencies to place themselves above others. Interestingly, after the small group discussions, the coaches noticed a notable improvement in the relationship between these two players to the point where they were choosing to warm up with one another, which had not happened prior to the discussion of the assessment results.

Understanding behavioral tendencies also helped me address issues between players on the field. Here is a message that I sent to one of my players after a conversation had occurred during a practice (names have been changed):

I sensed from our conversation last night that you may be challenged playing with Jules in the back. I would like you to look at the attached team report that we discussed together early in the season. It may help to explain some of the struggles that may be occurring. Specifically look at where you and Jules plot on the Team Wheel . . . the characteristics that you and Jules have are similar to Ron (Bonnstetter) and I. Ron is the person that has provided us with the TriMetrix® DNA instrument and he is a conductor. Many people struggle dealing with Ron because he is direct, will take aggressive action, and will appear to become angry quickly. He thrives on change. This is Jules. In contrast, I like to do things systematically, diplomatically, and do not like things to change too quickly. I have learned to adapt to his style and we have become very good friends. I am sure he has adapted to my style as well . . . . As I indicated last night, we need to focus on what we can control, that is in this case, how we go about adapting to others. It is not easy, but in the big picture it is a valuable skill that requires practice. I do not have any expectations that you will become BFFs (Best Friends Forever) with Jules, but it is important that you recognize your differences with Jules as you interact on the field. She may come across as angry and impatient especially if she is under stress. One of the reasons I have Jules in the middle back is to take advantage of her conductor style.

From a coaching perspective, attempting to change your defensive system of play to meet the needs of a given game situation may meet resistance if your backs have characteristics of coordinators. Furthermore, if you have expectations that your backs are going to need to be loud communicators, then a coordinator may be very much challenged by this. It is not that they cannot be loud, it is just that it is going to take a very concerted effort on their part to be able to overcome their more natural tendencies. Persuaders are typically more animated and come across as being extroverted in contrast to the coordinators, who will be introverted and very reserved during their interactions with each other. The coordinators will keep their emotions to themselves. From a coaching perspective, coordinators need to be given an environment where they will have the opportunity to directly and openly express their feelings and concerns. When facing challenges such as being down at half time one to nil, the persuaders will be saying "We can do it" whereas the coordinators will be asking "How do we do it?" In the context of receiving instruction, coordinators need specific instruction, follow-up, and follow-through.

When I have the information available, I do my best to assess the top two motivators for individual players. This will increase the likelihood of getting the player more engaged and moving into action. For example, I have often struggled with players whose primary or secondary driver is the individualistic motivator, because they want to be in charge and have decision-making authority. Although it took me awhile to figure it out, I learned that if I provide them with opportunities to lead and do it their way as well as solicit their input on decisions, the team functioned a lot smoother and our relationship became more collaborative. In the case of the soccer team in the story, over 71% of these players have social as their primary or secondary motivator. They want a team environment that has minimal conflict and is in harmony. As a coach whose top two motivators are fundamentally different, it is extremely important that I be open to dealing with subjectivity and feelings and the extent to which I assert my decision-making authority. If the culture of the team is not meeting the motivational needs of the player, this will increase the likelihood of a player leaving and looking elsewhere for a team that meets their needs.

As previously noted, one of the primary purposes for giving the players the assessment was to help each player gain a better understanding of self. By increasing their understanding of self and their teammates, the goal was to help them to develop strategies to meet the demands of the environment; that is, being a member of the team. The following is an example of how one player gained a better understanding of self and, from my perspective, made the entire exercise worthwhile regardless of the extent to which the rest of the team benefitted. It clearly had a positive impact on her.

So, before the season even started, I could've told you that I always followed rules. In my eyes, as the TriMetrix® DNA report said, I see rules as being there to follow. However, I saw this as more of a "party-pooper/ too uptight" thing. And I didn't really see that it was okay. I thought it was more of a negative quality, when really it could've been a strength. I also learned that I can be stubborn at times. When I first saw that on the TriMetrix report, I immediately regarded it as totally wrong, but when I thought about it, it can be very true. I'm not necessarily someone that will totally regard the opinions of others as wrong, but I can still be stubborn. The report also said that I was pessimistic which really didn't float my boat at the time, so I worked hard to fix that in case it was a problem. And, according to my teammates, my hard work is paying off. Also, I learned and am still learning, even outside of soccer, that I'm motivated by my values. If you had asked me that before the report, I probably would've told you that my motivation was along the lines of 'I'll do this because I don't want to get in trouble.'

From an educational perspective, knowing the behavioral styles of my students has been helpful for me and the students in the management of small groups on a semester-long project (Figure 11). In the use of these instruments, I continually emphasize that none of these characteristics are right or wrong, simply different behavior and motivational styles; all of which can be used for an effective team.

Forty-seven students are plotted on a team wheel. As discussed in the caption for Figure 5, each person has a different pattern of DISC relative to the energy line, which is the horizontal centerline, in all the small embedded graphics on Figure 11. The pattern associated with a person whose C dominates has a C score high above the energy line and D, I, S are below the line. The core behavioral style is the highest point plotted above the energy line. The point spread between each of the behavioral dimension scores influences the tendencies for a certain behavior. Each one of the numbered boxes on Figure 11 represents different DISC patterns. The inset graphs provide examples for areas 1, 6, 12, 15, 20, and 21.

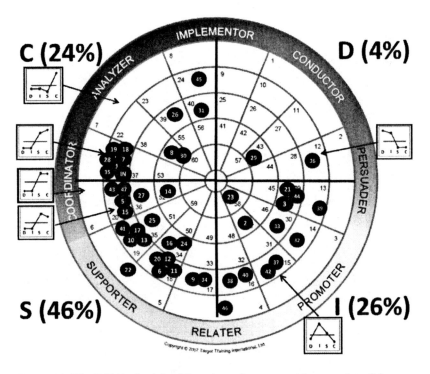

Figure 11. The DISC wheel for 47 students. Insets provide examples of the patterns of D, I, S, and C for specific areas on the wheel. Each numbered area on the graph represents a distinct DISC pattern similar to those illustrated in Figure 5. Each numbered dot represents a student. The IN represents instructor Gosselin. Purpose of graph is to illustrate behavioral differences across the class. Used with permission from the author and publisher, Target Training International.

The primary reason for using the DISC wheel in this class was to help improve communication among the members of working groups that were formed based only on their interest in a particular environmental issue. Using the wheel, the team members shared their styles with each other, and used some team-blending resources to recognize, understand and appreciate the different behavioral styles. The team-blending resources provided details regarding each group member's strengths, weaknesses, problem-solving abilities, and communication preferences for each of the eight general categories— conductor, persuader, etc., provided on the outside of the wheel.

Another important application of the DISC wheel is to help students develop one of the most important skills students need to acquire to be successful at any level of an organization: the ability to effectively interact with other people. "Over 80% of the people who move up in corporations are promoted because of their people skills, NOT technical ability."[16] As part of our classroom debriefing sessions, we directly addressed our individual tendencies to assume that everyone interacts and thinks the same way we do. This assumption can result in a breakdown of interactions among group members shortly after the group is formed. Our data in Figure 11 clearly indicates substantial behavioral differences among the students in the class and between students and the instructor (labeled IN in Figure 11).

A primary takeaway message from the soccer team story and the example from an educational setting is that there can be significant differences between the instructor and the students, coaches and players, and among the students and players themselves in the context of behavioral and motivational drivers. These differences are certainly in the workplace as well. These differences need to be explicitly addressed because they will impact the effectiveness of the individuals and the organization, whether it is a soccer team, a group in a class, or a business.

Having knowledge of the motivational and behavioral characteristics of even the youngest members of the community with which you are engaged will influence the process of how you are going to take them along on the journey. For example, having knowledge that children play sports for a variety of reasons that includes that they want to:

- learn and improve
- have fun
- be with friends
- compete
- get fit; and develop skills

These motivators should influence the design and implementation of coaching of all sports at the youth level. Note that competing is important, not necessarily the outcome-oriented win versus loss that seems to haunt parents and coaches. In the business world, addressing these differences is critical in the context of adapting for success among employees and between employees, and their leaders.

Having knowledge of the motivational drivers and behavioral characteristics of the people you are trying to influence on their journey to someplace new will help you more effectively interact with them. In addition, helping a person understand themselves has rewards, in and of itself, that go well beyond the soccer pitch, classroom, or office, and hopefully contribute to the long-term success of the player, student, or employee in the game of life. This, of course, leads to a more positive experience for everyone on the team as conveyed by one of my players in a late season email:

Being honest, at the beginning of the season, I really wasn't looking forward to this whole bonding, getting-to-know-each-other stuff. I thought that we were better off spending our time working on soccer and not learning about each other. . . . However, looking back, you can see that I was obviously soooooo wrong. And I guess that going through that really helped me respect you more as a coach (not that I didn't respect you already, or anything). Also, when all of us were just out there in the open, it helped us bond so much more and I am so much closer to this team then I thought was possible at the beginning of the season. And bonding obviously led to better and more positive interaction. . . . Like I said earlier, if you had asked me at the beginning of the season, I would've told you that this would've been a waste of time. However, it has helped tremendously. As players, and as friends, we understand and respect each other better. And the feeling goes out from everybody for everybody. No teammate is excluded from this.

AGE

It is very important to know and understand the physical, emotional, and mental characteristics of the players, students, and employees for whom you are responsible. For example, understanding the characteristics of our players, as in any educational activity, will help us create a developmentally appropriate training and learning environment for them. Table 3 highlights the different stages of cognitive/brain development for humans. Clearly children have different abilities than adults.

Table 3. Piaget's cognitive development stages.[17]

Stage	Age	Characteristics of Stage
Sensorimotor	0-2	Child learns by doing; looking, touching, sucking, primitive understanding of cause and effect relationships.
Preoperational	2-7	Child uses language and symbols, including letters and numbers. Egocentrism is also evident. Conservation marks the end of the preoperational stage and the beginning of the concrete operations.
Concrete	7-11	Child demonstrates conservation, reversibility, serial ordering, and mature understanding of cause and effect relationships. Thinking at this stage is concrete.
Formal operations	12+	Individual demonstrates abstract thinking, including logic, deductive reasoning, comparison, and classification.

Children younger than age ten can have a considerable range in playing ability and physical maturity. Physically mature individuals demonstrate stronger motor skills. A coach's tendency will be to focus on the more capable players. You may not think that players notice but they do. I can give you many examples. One of the most recent was a friend of mine telling me about his daughter's experience with her coach. The daughter made the observation that her coach seemed to consistently point out the good things two of the better players did. She felt that the coach only seemed to point out the things she did wrong. Her perception is her reality.

Recognizing that you may have this tendency is the first step to dealing with this potential problem. Another concrete step is to do your best to recognize at least one positive thing each player does during training. For young players, this might be something as simple as recognizing a player for getting their socks over their shin guards for the first time. Whatever recognition or feedback you give needs to be meaningful and sincere, otherwise it will lose its effectiveness over time.

Also be aware about discussing concepts that your players or students may not have the ability to understand because of their age. A prime example of this is telling six-year-olds to spread out and use the space on a soccer field. This seems obvious to us as adults. However, the brains of the vast majority of six-year-olds are not developed to the point where an abstract concept like space can be understood. So regardless of how many times you tell them, they will generally gravitate back to the most concrete concept on the field and, that is, to get the ball. Hence, you end up with the beehive around the ball. Another example is telling a story about never leaving your wingman like in the movie *Top Gun*, related to defending in soccer, when your players have never heard of the movie.

I always tell one story to coaches about a game of micro soccer I was watching one Saturday afternoon. The five-year-olds were out on the field chasing the ball in the classic beehive shape. The parents were all providing directions from the side lines. The coaches, who also served as on-field referees, were also watching and encouraging the players to make space. One of the coaches walked into the beehive, picked up one of the players like a chess piece, moved him away from the bunch, and set him down away from the group.

That player hardly moved from that spot for the rest of the game. The game was no longer fun and I suspect he did not play too much longer after that.

GENERATIONAL DIFFERENCES

Just as the case is in business, you may find yourself coaching, teaching, and employing people across generational divides. The students who are graduating from college now are entering a workforce in which there could be four generations working for the same company. This is challenging and at the same time exciting. However, it is important to confront two fundamental assumptions that each generation makes about the younger generations entering a given organization. Cam Marston, in his 2007 book, *Motivating the 'What's in it for Me' Workforce,*[18] highlights these two assumptions. First, the senior generation in an organization assumes that the younger generations will measure success the same way they did. Second, the senior generation also believes that the younger ones entering their organization should pay their dues and follow the same pathways to achieve success that they did. Regardless of the generation, success, time, work ethic, styles and types of communication, experience with technology, and self-efficacy are valued in different ways.

As a fifty-something, I am from the baby boomer generation. I am coaching, teaching, and employing people who are generally twelve to twenty-four years old. This age group is defined as being the late millennial, Y, or Z generation, depending on the source categorizing the generations.[19] Regardless of how you refer to them, on a daily basis I have to continually attempt to adapt to their characteristics. Some of the more challenging elements of their styles for me are that while they are apparently good at multitasking, they are challenged to have an old fashioned, face-to-face conversation. Telephone conversations are just as challenging. Texting is a very important, and for some, the only form of communication. They also give you the impression that their time is more important than yours. They seek convenience for them in things they do and there does seem to be a sense of entitlement among them. All these characteristics in and of themselves are not bad things. They are just different. However, the differences need to be managed when working across the generational boundaries, if you are going to effectively harness the skills of a multigenerational workforce and help move people forward to new places. We need to be very aware of the different lenses and filters that the different generations use when dealing with the world and people around them. It may also be useful to put these differences out there for discussion. Putting it out there will make all sides more aware of it, which in the long run will hopefully improve the opportunity for better communication and relationship development. Do not hesitate to search the web to keep up to date on generational differences.

GENDER DIFFERENCES

I have always coached young women. One of the primary reasons is nicely summarized by Anson Dorrance, winner of twenty-one NCAA National Championships as the women's coach at the University of North Carolina, and also the coach of the UNC's men's squad early in his career, who said, "You basically have to drive men, but you can lead women. . . . The way you coach women is a more civilized mode of leadership. If you read any books about the leadership styles of men and women, you learn that the men's style is a hierarchical style. It is a very top-to-bottom structure. A woman's style is more like a network."[20] Helgeson and Johnson, in their 2010 book *The Female Vision: Women's Real Power at Work,*[21] highlight that women and men experience the world in different ways and have different tendencies that influence how they act and react in various situations. Women tend to be more empathetic, more aware of the critical impact of interpersonal factors both within and without the organization. They prefer to connect with everyone and will relate to people on a more emotional level. It is about building relationships. Men on the other hand tend to exclude emotion and empathy during their interactions with others. For men it is commonly about the bottom line and using a sharply focused, linear way of thinking. To get something from a team of men, demanding it will be far more effective with them than it will be with women, who are looking to be influenced through an effective leadership relationship.

Both perspectives are important. We just need to recognize that these differences need to be considered in group dynamics and moving forward. From a coaching and leading perspective, males need to be cognizant of feelings and relationships. Because of our cultural environment, this is not necessarily an easy task for males, but we need to confront the challenges to create an environment where all can be as successful as they want to be.

KNOWLEDGE AND SKILL SETS

Many assumptions are made about what students, players, and employees know and what they can do. We all know what happens when we assume. From a brain-based approach, it is important to know where people are starting from, before we try to take them someplace new. In the context of an educational setting, we need to assess the knowledge and understanding of our students on a given topic, before moving forward. At its most basic level, finding out what your students know about a topic may be as simple as having them take out a piece of paper and asking them some very simple questions about the topic. You may find out that many of them have a good handle on the topic at hand and that to spend significant time on a topic is actually a waste of everyone's time and resources. You may also learn about their misconceptions. Accessing previous knowledge is important to constructing new knowledge. On the other hand, if we assume that students can do something or know something and they cannot, this can lead to frustrations on both sides of the classroom.

One of the biggest challenges that higher education faces is preparing today's students to meet future workforce demands. Business and political leaders are increasingly asking schools, including institutions of higher education, to develop personal skills/professional competencies such as innovation, creativity, problem solving, critical thinking, communication, collaboration, and self-management, among others (Table 4). In their book, *The Complete Leader,*[22] Ron Price and Randy Lisk provide an articulate accounting regarding the competencies that leaders need to be successful. Through the use of an instrument such as the TTI TriMetrix (such as in Figure 4), our Environmental Studies program at the University of Nebraska–Lincoln is taking a page from the business world to both identify student needs and, in turn, improve programs of study that include and emphasize opportunities to enhance professional competency. Through the use of these types of instruments, we know what skill sets students have when they leave the program.

Having this information has been very valuable for the students during their job search.

Table 4. Twenty-three competencies assessed using the TTI Performance DNA™ system and categorized using the domains identified by the National Research Council. Table from Gosselin and others, 2013.[23]

Domains from National Research Council	TTI Performance DNA Competencies
Cognitive Competencies: n=5	Planning and organizing Analytical problem solving Decision making Creativity/innovation Futuristic thinking
Intrapersonal Competencies: n=5	Continuous learning Goal orientation Self-management Flexibility Personal effectiveness
Interpersonal Competencies: n=13	Employee development/coaching Presenting Diplomacy Management Customer service Interpersonal skills Leadership Teamwork Conflict management Empathy Persuasion Written communication Negotiation

MINDSET

Another important attribute that needs to be considered is the mindset of your players, students, and employees. The concept of mindsets has been developed by psychologist Dr. Carol Dweck and discussed in her 2006 book, *Mindset: The New Psychology of Success*.[24] Dweck identifies two mindsets—a "growth mindset" and a "fixed mindset." Focusing on effort, specifically persistent effort, is important for our players, students, and employees to have success on the field, in the classroom, and beyond. Focusing on the development of persistent effort relates to a mindset that recognizes success is based on hard work, learning, training, and perseverance. For people who have this type of mindset, which is a growth mindset, they realize their performance can always be improved, and learning comes from making mistakes. Mistakes come from doing and so does success. These types of people focus on the questions of "How can I get better and what do I have to do?"

As a coach, educator, and employer, I want players who have the growth mindset, in contrast to those who have a fixed mindset. People with fixed mindsets believe they have been born with an innate talent and ability and that these traits are fixed. These people often have a fear of making mistakes because they feel it makes a negative statement about their abilities and themselves.

We can help those who lead to develop the growth mindset, but it takes practice on our part. I try to do several things with both my players and students to help them develop a growth mindset. I continuously emphasize that their focus should be on doing their best and improving, as these are things they have control over and can take charge of. I encourage them to take charge and responsibility for their success, and to look at setbacks as motivation to improve.

I would encourage you to read Dweck's book. It is well written in a straightforward manner with lots of helpful hints. At this point I will leave you with a quote from Dr. Dweck that will give you something to ponder.

> In a fixed mindset students believe their basic abilities, their intelligence, their talents, are just fixed traits. They have a certain amount and that's that, and then their goal becomes to look smart all the time and never look dumb. In a growth mindset students understand that their talents and abilities can be developed through effort, good teaching and persistence. They don't necessarily think everyone's the same or anyone can be Einstein, but they believe everyone can get smarter if they work at it.

CHAPTER 5

What Does the End Look Like?

To begin with the end in mind means to start with a clear understanding of your destination. It means to know where you're going
so that you better understand where you are now so that the
steps you take are always in the right direction.

- Stephen R. Covey, *The Seven Habits of Highly Effective People*

So you know yourself a little bit better and have some idea of the
characteristics of those players, students, and employees who for a
variety of reasons have joined you on this journey to somewhere
new. Now you have to decide the destination for your journey. On
a personal level, you have already done this, probably many times,
as you have planned various aspects of your life. You have developed certain ideas regarding ends you have had in mind and you
didn't even realize it. When you think about it, this is an incredibly
smart way to look to the future, by looking at the end first and then
working your way backwards. You have not only done goal setting,
you have developed a standard or raised the bar to the next level.
Once you have established that new target level, then you start
working your way slowly toward the end goal until you achieve it

or even surpass it. Because this is your destiny, you are able to mold it any way that you would like.

The same approach works to define the destination for your team. It creates a direction for the team. It channels and focuses its energy and talents. It creates expectations. Whether you are a coach, a teacher, or a business professional, you need to have a destination, an end in mind. Starting with the end in mind is a common and very effective approach to developing a plan so you get where it is you want to end up.

The bottom line—all successful leadership journeys start with the end in mind. The end is our goal.

A FAMILY TRIP METAPHOR

In our daily lives, think of all the ways we imagine something first (the end) and then do the planning. The process by which a family trip is planned is a great analogy for this end-in-mind strategy. To implement a family trip, defining the destination is the first step. This is the end you have in mind. To start off, you might ask yourself (or your family) what type of vacation experience you want. Do you want the experience to be an action-packed whirlwind, or do you want tranquil, low maintenance, and stress free? If you pick the former, you may be gearing up to head to Disney World and experience all the related theme parks. If it's the latter, you'll head to the lake cabin in northern Minnesota. Either way, the destination represents a strategic goal—the end you have in mind. If the end you have in mind—your vacation goal—is Disney World, then a whole series of questions arise that need to be answered to increase the probability of successfully achieving your goal.

Questions about the resources you will need: money, transportation? How long do you plan to stay? How long will it take to travel to and from your town of origin? Based on this series of questions, among many others that could be asked, some specific objectives (or actions) are established that will need to be completed if you are going to successfully meet your goal. A couple of examples might be: Objective 1. Create a financial assessment of the cost of a five-day trip to Disney World including transportation and assets to pay for the trip; Objective 2. Develop trip itinerary including travel time, daily visits to the park, restaurants, etc. You get the point.

It is extremely important that you plan a family trip. Of course, as is the case with most planning efforts, there are more people involved than just you. One way to make the plan is for the destination to be defined autocratically by the parents who declare that Disney World is the goal. An autocratic approach may be fairly effective when your children are young and do not have the capacity or the background knowledge to realistically contribute to the decision-making process. However, for anyone who has pre-teens and teenagers, making the choice not to seek input from this group, who will be directly impacted by your choice, may lead to disastrous consequences. I remember a family vacation as a teenager, in which we drove 5,501 miles in three weeks. All decisions about destinations and time spent were made without input from everyone who would be traveling. Needless to say, it was a very long three weeks and turned out to be our last family vacation.

A more effective strategy for planning uses a collaborative approach, seeking input from everyone who has a stake in the success of the vacation. Using strategic planning vernacular, you should engage your stakeholders. To employ a collaborative approach, the parents would seek input from all members of the family team to create a shared vision for the trip. This provides opportunities for each member of the team to contribute their ideas, and creates an opportunity to combine the different perspectives, knowledge, skills, talents, and ideas of everyone involved. Through this process, all participants have the opportunity to contribute, cooperate, and compromise through a collective effort. Of course, as in any planning process, there are constraints. In this family trip scenario, the age and hence experience of the children will come into play, in terms of their abilities to genuinely contribute ideas. Resources, i.e., family budget, may influence the choices available. The amount of vacation time available to a parent from their job may place additional constraints. Considering the constraints and contributions from each family member will result in buy-in from the entire family and increase the probability that the vacation plan will be a success.

QUESTIONS TO GET YOU TO THE END YOU HAVE IN MIND

Planning with the end in mind is a form of backwards design (Wiggins and McTighe, 2013).[25] One of the simplest approaches to this planning strategy is to ask a couple of questions to start the process. These are, "what do you want them to know" and/or "what will they be able to do?" These will help you identify the end goal.

However, I think it serves the process to give context to the knowing, doing, and what they will gain in terms of personal qualities, as they go through the process. So, as we move forward from here a more comprehensive set of questions will be used to help develop a plan with an end in mind. These are the four basic questions (BQ):

BQ1: What are you preparing them for?
BQ2: What will they know?

BQ3: What will they be able to do?

BQ4: What personal qualities will they possess?

Use the answers to these questions to build a complete picture of the end goal, addressing each question in the context of coaching, educating, and employing. The thought process is represented in Figure 12.

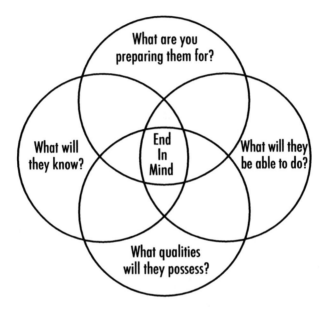

Figure 12. Questions used to focus the development of the end in mind. Copyright by David Gosselin, Ph.D.

PLANNING THE PLAN – COACHING CONSIDERATIONS

As a coach considering BQ1, it's important to put the end goal in the context of what you are preparing your players for. You might think the answer to this question is simple, but based on my coaching experiences, it is not.

When I first started coaching soccer, I was responsible for a recreational youth team of eight-year-old girls. We had a ten-week
season where we had one, one-hour training session and one 50-
minute game each week. Although we had a fall and spring season,
there was no guarantee that the teams would have the same group
of players from the fall season to the spring season. So, what was I
preparing them for? At the time, I thought I was preparing them
to become soccer players, but as I reflect back on this experience,
I hope I was preparing them to have fun, get some exercise, and
enjoy the game of soccer.

When several of the girls on this recreational team reached twelve
years old, we moved into a more competitive league where teams
played and stayed together for both fall and spring seasons. We had
two to three training sessions and a game each week. As I reflected
on the end in mind, I came to the realization that I was preparing
my players to be successful at the high school level. I think it should
be clear that the answer to BQ1 for the recreational compared to
the competitive team is distinctively different. I was preparing the
players on my competitive team for a very different end in mind,
compared to many other competitive coaches, who were preparing
their players to play in college or on elite, competitive club teams.

For questions BQ2 and BQ3, how do you know the appropriate
answers to the questions, *What do you want them to know?* and
What will they be able to do? For soccer, when I was serving as the
director of coaching for the YMCA Spirit Soccer Club, I compiled
a player development guide from a variety of sources, including the
National Soccer Coaches Association of America and U.S. Youth
Soccer, along with other published resources. These types of guides
provide the foundation for answering these questions. An example
is provided in Table 5.

Table 5. Soccer techniques and tactics for typical 9- and 10-year-olds. Player
development guide compiled for YMCA Spirit Soccer Club.
Copyright by David Gosselin, Ph.D.

Player Characteristics:
- Players are developing ability to focus longer and stay on task.
- Significant improvement in memory.
- Significant physical differences exist.
- Association with team increasingly important.
- They are active learners.
- Coordination improves.
- Peer group pressure becomes significant.
- Ability to think in advance of ball begins.

Strategies:
- Continue to emphasize mastery of stage 2 skills.
- Explanations brief and concise (less than 30 seconds).
- Begin to link activities with technical and tactical abilities of the players.
- Build on their experiences and provide them opportunities to solve problems on the field.
- Players learn better when they are given the opportunity to resolve problems on their own without the help of the coach.
- Ask them questions to promote problem solving.
- Keep things simple.

Techniques:
- Speed dribbling
- Heading
- Applying defensive pressure
- Driven balls - instep drive and outside of foot
- Receiving ground and bouncing balls with inside and outside of foot
- Develop ability to turn on an opponent
- Introduce crossing

Tactics:
- Players begin to think of, or anticipate the ball. They start to recognize when and where to move with and without the ball. Introduce 1 v 1 defending; roles of 1st attacker and defender; 2 v 1; attacking two player combination - overlap, wall pass, take-over, etc.; possession (4 v 1; 3 v 1, 4 v 2).

As in any educational activity, these types of guides will assist you in creating a developmentally appropriate plan for your players. This guide emphasizes a model for mastering soccer techniques and tactics in four basic stages. Although a typical age is assigned to a given stage, the age at which a player moves from one stage to the next depends on how old they are when they start playing the game. The new-to-the-game players I've had on my high school team have to progress through the stages just like a seven-year-old. Moving from one stage to the next in the context of the basic techniques is dependent on:

- The time players spend with the ball, both at training and practicing on their own.

- Player experience in previous stages, in terms of time spent on the ball and mastering related techniques.

- Taking no shortcuts! Each stage is vital and a prerequisite to the next stage.

- Physical and intellectual characteristics of the player. Each player will progress through the stages differently. In some areas, players who start playing at an older age may progress more quickly through some parts of specific stages because their brains are better developed.

Successful progression with respect to the tactical part of the game, or making and implementing choices, is dependent on the current level of skill. Simply put, tactics cannot be developed without technical skill.

The stage development model is very consistent with what Dr. Ronald Quinn, Head Women's Soccer Coach at Xavier University and noted soccer clinician, has articulated about player development and time. The following quote from Dr. Quinn really captures the philosophy that I try to convey to any coaches I've had an opportunity to train:

> From the perspective of player development, we must embrace the viewpoint that growth is a process. Players do not develop in just one season; it takes several years. Unfortunately, many young players are either selected out, or drop out at too early an age, largely because playing is no longer enjoyable.

I certainly wish I had been exposed to these pearls of wisdom from Dr. Quinn and also had access to the guide such as the one in Table 5. It might have made things easier. However, I probably would not have recognized the importance of the message early in my coaching career because just as players go through developmental stages, so do coaches. I suspect I would not have been ready to take advantage of either resource.

I want to really emphasize the importance of time on task (i.e., time with the ball) and repetition when considering your season plan. When training coaches to put their season plan together, I emphasize the importance of technique repetition and using different training designs so that the technique becomes a skill.

A technique becomes a skill when a player can use the technique in the context of a game situation.

Based on my years of observation, a group of players must experience at least three training sessions to get at least 25% of them transitioning the technique into a skill. I would be curious to see someone test this hypothesis.

One of the most important services I believe a coach can provide to his players is opportunities to address BQ4, *What personal qualities will they possess?* This may be better phrased as, what personal qualities do you, as a coach, want to help your players develop? The qualities referred to in this question are part of what is known as the affective domain, which includes such things as attitudes, appreciation, values, emotions, biases, etc. The personal qualities that the players on my high school team set forth as being important are referred to as the Lady Warrior Way, and include:

- We play with integrity according to our Christian values.
- We believe in, care for, and respect our teammates. Everyone brings something to the team!
- We choose to be positive.
- We compete with pride and determination! Effort makes the individual, the team, and the program successful.
- We are committed to our academic success.
- We have fun! Play and enjoy the game.

PLANNING THE PLAN – EDUCATIONAL CONSIDERATIONS

I have spent a considerable amount of time training, working with, and learning from K-12 educators and colleagues from teacher preparation programs. I have benefitted tremendously from their expertise over the years. These groups are responsible for driving my interest in helping people learn. They introduced me to the concept of planning the plan, so to speak. For K-12 educators, the "end" in mind is very much defined by various levels of standards that are issued at the school district, state, and/or federal level. For example, the Common Core Standards or New Generation Science Standards are "end-in-mind" documents. These standards-based documents are developed based on input from many stakeholders that, in general, address the 4 BQs I advocate here. I will focus on the planning process within higher education, with which I am intimately involved.

Prior to my work with my educational colleagues and a project designed to develop collaboration between K-12 teachers and faculty researchers,[26] I never really thought of college teaching as being part of curriculum or being driven by a curriculum development process. Nor did the faculty researchers involved in the project, all of whom taught college courses. I considered the development of a class in the same way that many in higher education do, that is, "I think we should start looking for a textbook that covers these topics," instead of using what I advocate here, which in educational vernacular is referred to as "backward design." As is the case in coaching, planning in higher education programs needs to address the same basic questions as part of the backward design process. For the parents of a prospective college undergraduate student, the question, "What end does your program have in mind for my son or daughter?" and the four basic questions of planning for the end in mind should be asked when exploring a major or program of study. The extent to which the program's representative can answer these questions will be quite telling, concerning the quality of the educational program their son or daughter—the student—will be involved in.

In higher education, we define the "end in mind" using a variety of terms including learning outcomes, learning goals, or learning objectives. These are commonly defined at the individual course level and up through various levels of academic programming. Regardless of the terminology (I will use learning outcomes), the "end in mind" needs to be defined in the context of the four basic questions highlighted earlier, related to knowledge, skills, and personal qualities the student will possess when they complete the educational program, in preparation for professional practice. Professional practice broadly defined includes workforce/career preparation, graduate and professional studies, and/or life-long learning. The "end" is typically a list of statements that describe significant and essential learning that the students will achieve and can reliably demonstrate at the end of the program.

BQ1, *What are you preparing them for?* has societal- and curriculum-focused overtones. Every program should be able to explicitly define what they are preparing their students for. Is the focus on career preparation for the professional workforce, or preparing them for graduate school, or preparing them for life-long learning, or all three?

Other questions that should be commonly addressed related to BQ1 include, "To what extent are students going to explicitly gain professional competency in teamwork, collaboration, problem solving, and futuristic thinking?" among others, as these are very important to professionals in the business world. To what extent is the program preparing students to address the societal needs of the local campus area, state, and nation? A focus on societal needs, designed into the curriculum, gives context to the educational elements of the program to which students can relate. This type of focus also demonstrates the commitment that higher education should have, to influence and improve people's lives beyond the borders of the university and its classrooms. I am a strong believer in this type of commitment as it can really set a university or college apart from its peers.

In the world of higher education, you would think developing an answer to address BQ2, *What will they know?* would be relatively straightforward, because the answer to the question is related to the facts, concepts, and theories central to the discipline. Many disciplinary areas have created discipline-related literacy documents that define what "everyone" should have some knowledge of. However, more and more, higher education is challenged by growth in interdisciplinary programs. For example, environmental studies, sustainability science, natural resources, and the list goes on. Defining what students should know in these areas is a matter of debate. Regardless, faculty in any related academic program should be involved in an ongoing discussion about what is the best answer to BQ2, in the context of their group expertise.

Developing an answer to BQ3, *What can they do?* involves similar caveats to that of BQ2. The answer should be continuously discussed. The answer to this question relates to behavioral and psychomotor components in three areas, and includes manual or physical skills:

1. Cognitive: critical thinking, problem-solving, computational skills.

2. Technical: data collection techniques, measurement techniques, technology.

3. Interpersonal: communication, writing, teamwork, collaboration, initiative, leadership.

The cognitive and technical skills are a strong focus for many programs, as they should be. However, the incorporation of curriculum elements for the development of interpersonal skills in the context of the specific disciplinary or interdisciplinary area is not as common as it should be. Context is important to learning many of these interpersonal skills, often referred to as "soft skills." I would argue that they are harder skills and take longer to learn than many of the technical and knowledge skills that are assumed to be important. Test this hypothesis by asking employers and I think you will be surprised. I know I was, after talking with employers at career fairs and exploring the literature related to the professional competencies employers are looking for.

Of the four basic questions, the least amount of time is probably spent on BQ4, *What personal qualities will they possess?* if it is considered at all. One reason for this lack of attention is that the outcomes, or answers, to this question relate to the affective domain—attitudes, appreciations, values, emotions, biases, etc. These are also referred to as value or disposition outcomes, and most faculty don't consider these as important, even though we actually try to encourage our students to grow these skills. Examples include:

- Open-mindedness
- Love of knowledge
- Willingness to learn and modify perspectives
- Desire to develop personal interests
- Willingness to take (intellectual) risks
- Diligence and integrity
- Perseverance in one's work habits

- Pursuit of quality results
- Humility about one's own importance; social responsibility
- Ethical awareness
- Appreciation for diversity

I am reasonably sure that no one would argue with these as being important and/or that we already encourage their development. By actually articulating them in learning outcomes, you raise them to a higher level and further demonstrate their importance to the students. Articulating them also shows that the development of the whole student in some type of value-based work is important.

A special note to my colleagues in higher education, especially those in administrative levels who want to use planning tools: it is unfortunate that when faculty hear the words planning, strategic planning, goal setting, etc., they seem to commonly respond with rolling of the eyes, an exasperated sigh, or an under-the-breath, "Here we go again." Part of the reason for this attitude stems from their experience with planning, which has not been positive. They have planned projects in the past that were never implemented. When follow-up related to implementation does not occur multiple times, the concept of planning loses value and is deemed a waste of time.

Building on the analogy of the family trip, if you invest time and energy in planning a vacation to Disney World, and then don't go through with it and don't follow up or explain why to your family members, you will lose credibility in your family's eyes. They will ignore you, or question your sincerity when it comes time next year to plan for the family vacation. To varying degrees, this has happened in higher education. Planning and goal setting have lost credibility at the faculty level, where these activities could do a lot of good. A key message here is that if people are going to invest in making plans or setting goals, follow-up and follow-through must occur—otherwise these efforts will be viewed as a waste of time.

PLANNING THE PLAN – BUSINESS CONSIDERATIONS

When considering the phrase "starting with the end in mind" in connection with business applications, this can mean a lot different things. Results of a Google search will yield a variety of different results, ranging from how to start a new business to Stephen Covey's context of providing personal direction to guide your daily activities toward personal success. My intended meaning is taking employees to someplace new, as an organizational group. Sometimes this place may be established by your corporate office and you need to figure out how to get there. Or, it could be that you are establishing the place through a planning process. In either case, a change process will be involved and hence a process of learning will need to be considered. As the manager or leader of your group, they are your team. You are going to help them move forward, similarly to the way a coach or teacher would. The four basic questions still apply and should be used as a guide for setting goals and expectations.

In your role with your employees, you need to build on what you have. To maximize their value to the company, you need to achieve buy-in for them to create win-win situations. In the 1999 book, *First, Break All the Rules: What the World's Greatest Managers Do Differently,*[27] Marcus Buckingham and Curt Coffman described a Gallup study that involved 80,000 managers in over 400 organizations. In this study, the number one answer to the question

"What do employees want?" was "To know what is expected of me at work." Working with employees to jointly develop expectations and ends-you-have-in-mind will help everyone know what they are to do. Setting these expectations with your employees will provide the foundation for more effective and collaborative performance management. If you can get buy-in at this level, you are on your way. I experienced this type of management years ago back when working in a produce department in a grocery store during high school and college. Reflecting back on the organization, I do not think that this type of management was done intentionally. I think this experience occurred more by accident than intent, but it had the same positive impact. The two managers for whom I worked during this time shared the expectations from upper management with our group. This set the expectations related to what we were preparing for. We were preparing to have the best profit margin of all the stores. We worked together to share and implement ideas regarding how we could improve the efficiency of our production to be sure we had plenty of product available on the shelves in a timely fashion. We also worked in an environment where we developed an attitude to strive to be the best and to work hard when we were there. We also had a lot of fun doing what we did. The take-home message is that the basic questions can be applied at all levels.

FINAL WORDS ON THE PROCESS

If it is not obvious, the success of developing your end-in-mind, your goals/objectives/outcomes, depends on the use of a participatory process that engages the people involved or who will be impacted. You need to engage the stakeholders. Engaging in a participatory approach generates trust and commitment, creates ownership, and ensures that the direction(s) you have chosen to go have been considered from multiple perspectives. The end results are decisions that are relevant, appropriate, feasible, and sustainable because they have multiple levels of support. Stakeholders who have been involved in the process are more likely to support its scaling up than those who had little input. The participatory process that you engage in to successfully develop your end-in-mind (your goals/objectives/outcomes) shares many elements of collaboration and learning as they will be described below.

From a coaching perspective, the key stakeholders are you (the coach), your assistants, and your players. Depending on the level you are coaching, parents may also be key stakeholders who need to be engaged in the process. This engagement is particularly important in dealing with questions related to BQ1, for what are you preparing their son or daughter? At this stage of planning the plan, I would encourage you as a coach to ask the players and the parents what they think the end should be. You may be pleasantly surprised at the usefulness of the feedback you will receive. Providing them voice and opportunity to have input into the plan will help increase buy-in from the parents and the players. This approach also helps identify where there may be significant differences of opinion, which then can be addressed. For example, there will be parents of eight-year-olds who think you are preparing their daughter to be a world class soccer player, when the reality is you want them to get some exercise and have a positive experience. On the other hand, as a coach your plan may be to develop these eight-year-olds into world class players while the parents just want them to have some fun kicking the ball around. Without question this engagement process will take time up front, but will save you time and a lot of headaches in the long run.

Using a planning-with-the-end-in-mind approach, in an educational vernacular, we need to establish what it is we want the students to be able to know and do by the time they complete the course or program. The development of the learning outcomes for a program should be collaborative. It should involve alumni, employers, faculty, students, and documents from well-regarded sources. Using this collaborative approach will yield a curriculum that is relevant to students who want to proceed into the professional world as well as the students who want to pursue further training in a graduate degree program. Once a collaborative set of learning outcomes is established that can serve multiple audiences, then learning activities and pedagogies can be explored that will help the students achieve them.

We can also use the organizational planning vernacular whereby an organization (i.e., an athletic team, a business, etc.) defines its mission, vision, goals, and objectives. Again, it is important to involve the stakeholders in the organization. Once the mission, vision, goals, and objectives are defined, we can create plans of action to achieve organizational success. Whether you use the educational or organizational context, you are defining where you want your team to be and/or where you want to take them. Combining the where-you-want-to-take-them information with the skills and assets of the team members, you can begin to establish the plan of attack to successfully meet your team goals, objectives, and outcomes. As part of this process, it is critical to provide opportunities for feedback and consensus building to develop trust among team members, to get buy-in from the team members, and, to various degrees, to meet the needs of all team members.

CHAPTER 6

How NOT to Get to the End-in-Mind: Start Assuming!

We make all sorts of assumptions because we don't
have the courage to ask questions.

– Miguel Ruiz, *The Four Agreements:
A Practical Guide to Personal Freedom*

You have to be careful what you think you know. Assumptions, you
see, even when based on sound research, can lead us astray.

– Simon Simek, *Start with Why: How Great Leaders
Inspire Everyone to Take Action*

I've done it. You've done it. We've all done it. We have made assumptions that killed the relationships that are necessary to get to the end we have in mind. Bottom line: assumptions kill.

You know where you want to take your people. You have an end in mind. Now it is time to develop a plan that consists of strategies and methods that will get you and your participants where you want to go. This sounds easy. You fish back into your memory and look for the ways that you had experienced coaching, teaching, etc. One of the first and foremost assumptions that we tell ourselves is, "It worked for me so it should work for them just as well." Unfortunately, like other assumptions, this one can get you into trouble. Let me give you some examples.

During graduate school in the mid-1980s, I had my first opportunity to coach. It was my wife's softball team. I coached the team for two seasons. The women I coached had various degrees of competitiveness, some similar to mine. I like to win. I assumed that we all had the same goal and same desire to win.

The first season was a lot of fun and we were successful in the context of wins and losses. We certainly won more than we lost and finished strong in the playoffs. The second season was a different situation. For the most part we had the same core group of players. We added a couple of new players, some who were highly competitive, and others not so much. We started the season off well, playing at a similar level as the previous season. Then the wheels seemed to fall off. They did not come off all at once. They came off slowly. We began to lose and continued to lose until we lost more than ten games in a row to end the season.

My biggest concern at that time was how I was being perceived as the coach. I focused on me. I took the losses very personally. My attitude grew negative. I did not express this attitude too much verbally, because I did not want to be like a few coaches I had experienced growing up. Instead, I showed my displeasure mostly through my body language, and I thought that this would make a difference. Well, it did not. Things only seemed to get worse. During this time, I spent literally hours trying to figure out what was wrong—looking for something or someone to blame, because that is how I had experienced things growing up. It certainly could not be my fault.

Reflecting back, I can now take responsibility that I was the primary cause for the downward spiral. During the first season I coached, I had no expectations. I took one game at a time. It was no big deal. However, as a result of our success during my first season, I had expectations as to how good we were going to be. In addition to the expectations, I felt as though the team and what they accomplished were a direct reflection on me as a person. When we started falling short of these expectations, I became frustrated. This frustration led to negative body language, which contributed to an overall negative environment. This whole thing had become about me and not the women I was coaching.

My coaching career resumed when I first started coaching soccer in response to my eight-year-old daughter's request to coach her team. As is the case with many parent coaches, this opportunity was interesting, to say the least, because I did not really know anything at all about soccer. I had played some pickup soccer in high school, but that was about it. So as many coaches did prior to all the web resources and online bookstores, I went to the library and got some books to learn the game of soccer and get some great "drills" for practice. Well, I got what I needed and went to my first practice on a blustery cold day in March. I went to the first practice and had a parent meeting like all the coaching books tell you to do. One of the first things I told the parents was that I really knew nothing about this game and that we would figure it out as went along. I am sure that inspired a lot of confidence amongst the parents.

The next thing I did with my practice plan in hand was divide the hour-long practice into four segments—stretching and run--ning, dribbling, passing, and shooting. The plan I had in mind was that after this short training session, these third-grade girls would be able to play—dribble, pass, shoot the ball, and understand the game like an adult.

Of course, they didn't. It wasn't because they didn't want to; they couldn't because they were eight-year-olds. I suspect I got a little frustrated and could not figure out why they didn't get it. I had been around adults so much that I figured these little ones could learn like an adult, and had the physical abilities to see and do. I certainly began to think far more about me and my frustration than I was thinking about the girls. When I left the field that day, I came to the realization that this "coaching gig" was not going to be quite as simple as I thought.

I think back on this first practice and I laugh. It amuses me now as to how quickly the whole thing became about me. It also never dawned on me at the time that there was a better strategy and/or method to help these young ones learn the game of soccer. I had never really asked the question.

So, after my inaugural spring season as a coach, I started to ask questions as to how I might do this coaching thing better. I have this tendency to want to learn, figure things out, and solve the problem at hand, as I am strongly driven by my theoretical motivator. So I began to attend coaching clinics through the local YMCA. These clinics provided me with some basics, but it was clear that I needed much more and this thing called coaching was not as easy as it looked. So, when I saw that the National Soccer Coaches Association of America (NSCAA) was offering the first of what turned out to be an extensive sequence of coaching education opportunities, I took advantage of it. Coaching became my passion. As I do when I get passionate about something, I wanted to learn and know more. I went on a quest to learn more about this business of coaching and eventually, after about ten years, I became a trainer and educator of coaches.

From the perspective of an educator, a number of experiences highlight the importance of recognizing the assumptions you make about how people learn, and assumptions you make when choosing what methods and strategies—referred to in education vernacular as pedagogy—you think will make you an effective educator.

Knowing how people learn can make the learning process more efficient and, most definitely, more enjoyable.

The following stories did not seem significant to me at the time, but when I think back they illustrate several things that many educators assume on a fairly common basis.

EXAMPLES OF ASSUMPTIONS THAT KILL

One of the first assumptions I had to deal with when I became a coach, and still do to some extent today as an educator of coaches, is the "First an Expert" assumption. This assumption, in the context of coaching, could also be referred to as the "First a Player" assumption, that is, before you can help others learn the game, you had to have played the game at a high level. A related assumption is that if you played the game, you can coach. An interesting corollary to the "First an Expert" assumption in higher education is that if you have a Ph.D. in a given discipline, then you will be an effective teacher and an effective academic leader.

All three of these assumptions are myths. For me, they have been dispelled through coaching education and working with colleagues in the education world. There are many examples of some very good coaches who have not played the game at a very high level. One of the reasons for this is that coaching and playing require a different set of skills, see Table 6. Bill Beswick's 2001 book, *Focused for Soccer: Developing a Winning Mental Approach,* described the skills needed to be a player and distinguished them from those of a coach.[28]

Table 6. The characteristics of coaches and players.

Player Characteristics	Coach Characteristics
• Physical skills (fitness) • Competitiveness • Technical skills • Tactical "sense" • Emotional skills • Imaging	• Leadership • Observation • Intellectual skill • Methodology • Communication

A key takeaway message is that training and coaching players is about helping them learn new skills. Coaching is all about designing the learning process to meet the needs of the players. Any learning process actually has stages of growth. Coaches need to use a range of methods and strategies relevant to the learning characteristics of the player and to the type of training that you are trying to provide: technical, tactical training, physical training/conditioning, and mental/psychological training. The learning process that you use is the vehicle to get your players where they want to go and where you as a coach want to help take them.

Another story from my graduate school days serves to illustrate the commonly-held assumption that having a significant amount of learning or research experience in a given field of study qualifies you to be an effective educator. In one of the last years of my Ph.D. program, I was asked to provide an educational experience for high school students on some of my research and interest in planetary geology. This was definitely an eye opener, when I think back, but I did not realize it at the time. As part of a NASA-related education day, I was asked to provide a 50-minute educational program on a topic of my choice. At the time, I was really into the moon and those circular features on its surface we can see on a clear night that are called impact craters.

I prepared the talk and gave it what I thought was a catchy title, the "Awesome Power of Meteorites." I had great slides. I felt I was well prepared. I gave my talk, showed them lots of cool of images of the moon, Earth, and other planets, and gave them some great statistics. I was energetic and enthusiastic. Periodically, looking at the audience of high school kids, it was clear they were not getting it. They were bored. Some were distracting each other by whispering and passing notes. I could not figure it out. How could they not think that what I was talking so passionately about was cool and interesting?

For years, I thought it was the high school kids who had the problem. I came up with many reasons for my lack of success, if you will. They were not paying attention. They did not care. They were not smart enough, among other reasons. Certainly, I was not the problem—but it turns out I was. The method and strategy (i.e., lecture) I used were ones I had experienced, and they worked for me. So I assumed they would work for them. As the old saying goes, when you assume, you know what happens. I definitely suffered the consequences for my assumption. The unfortunate thing is that not only have we experienced the consequence of similar assumptions made by teachers and professors throughout our educational careers, current students suffer the same consequences from similar assumptions.

If I knew then what I know now, I certainly would have approached this educational opportunity differently in terms of my methods and strategies to get them where I wanted them to go—that is, being able to describe the importance of impact cratering in landscape development in the early solar system. I did not know at the time that roughly only five percent of people learn effectively when lectured at, and that most people have attention spans of about ten minutes. After that, you should stop or change your mode of information delivery. Of course, I learn effectively through a lecture mode of information delivery. I assumed everyone else did as well. My choice of educational delivery was based on an incorrect assumption that if it works for me, then it will work for them.

A few years later in the early '90s, I had another experience that significantly impacted my assumptions about how I approached educational opportunities and the use of appropriate learning methods and strategies. I was asked to conduct two 90-minute sessions on groundwater and what was in it. My audience was a group of fifth graders. By this point in my career, I was starting to think about who the audience was and how I was going to reach them. However, although I had started to give it some thought, it was hard to give up old habits, so I went down the same path that I had with the high school students . . . creating a "great" slideshow presentation that would be the core of my educational offering. Fortunately, this time I brought a couple of "hands-on" activities. During the first session, I did my slide show and gave them a couple of paper mapping activities. These went okay, but I was really struggling to keep the students' attention. So I brought out my simple "hands-on" activities, involving some cups of water and different materials: salt, sand, and baking soda. These saved the day. We did some simple measuring with a spoon, put the materials in the water, and looked at what happened. We spent the last twenty minutes or so talking about solubility and how it influences what is in their drinking water. This was such a simple activity, but it connected them with stuff they already knew. The activity focused their attention and drew connections between the concepts I presented and everyday knowledge and experience they all had.

The moral of all these stories is that I had an end in mind where I wanted to take my wife's softball team, my daughter's soccer team, those high school students, and a group of fifth graders. Unfortunately, I did not know how to get them there. My first mistake, among many, in all four situations was that I made assumptions. I assumed my audiences were like me—they were interested and they learned the same way that I did. I was most definitely looking at me instead of considering those I was trying to reach. In the case of the eight-year-old soccer players, these young ladies were probably interested, but they certainly did not have the same capacity to learn as I did. This seems rather obvious, but it is only obvious if you take the time to think about those you are teaching. I guess I thought they were "mini-mes," so to speak. Sorry, I meant I assumed they were like me. In the case of the high school students, they were probably not too interested and they also did not learn like me—i.e., having someone talk at me seemed to work for me. Unfortunately, it did not work for them. My assumptions clearly did not allow me to make the right connections.

A key takeaway message is that to get to your end-in-mind, you must leave your assumptions at the door.

No matter how hard I try, I still catch myself making assumptions, but hopefully not as often. I keep practicing to leave them at the door because practice makes perfect.

CHAPTER 7

How to Get to the End-in-Mind: How People Learn + Collaboration

Although I did not realize it at the time, an educational project funded by the National Science Foundation entitled, "Using Earth Science Research Projects to Develop Collaboration Between Scientists at a Research University and K-12 Educators," had a profound and long lasting influence on me as an educator, coach, and leader. The project, completed in the early 2000s, forced me to develop a deeper understanding of collaboration and really launched me down the path to wanting to learn more about how people learn and how to integrate that knowledge into the learning experiences I was trying to provide.

There is no question in my mind that the integration of collaboration and an understanding of learning will have a profound impact on your abilities to achieve your end-in-mind.

We will address how people learn and collaborate separately, then we will bring them together to show how you can use these concepts to move people forward more effectively and more efficiently.

CHANGE INVOLVES A LEARNING PROCESS

It turns out that achieving the end you have in mind in some way, shape, or form will involve change. It is crucial to recognize that, whether you are a coach trying to help your player learn a new skill, an educator helping a student obtain new knowledge or skills, or an employer wanting to move their employees and business to a new place, all of these activities involve change. Change involves learning, whether we are doing something new or trying to do something better. We have all seen it. Learning can happen subtly, where we hardly notice it is occurring, or it can happen rapidly, when we have a learning experience that yields dramatic changes. In either case, learning is required for change to occur. Therefore, getting to the end in mind and reaching our goals requires us as coaches, educators, and business leaders to use methods and strategies that will engage people in learning so they can change and move forward.

Recent developments in educational research and cognitive science provide important and relevant insights into the learning process that are useful in terms of maximizing the effectiveness of our players, students, and employees. Regardless of the situation, the principles of learning apply.

Zull (2004) provides a straightforward description of what we know about the brain and learning. A very simplified way to view the brain is that it can be divided into four major regions.[29] Each region has different functions: *sensory cortex* (gathers information); *integrative cortex near the sensory cortex* (makes meaning of information); *integrative cortex in the front of the brain* (creates new ideas from these meanings); and *motor cortex* (acts on those ideas).

The more areas of the brain that are engaged by the learning process, the more neurons connect and the more neural networks change—and therefore more learning occurs.[30] Data and information enter a person's brain through concrete experience, but it is not until they have worked with these data and information and transformed it into their own ideas, plans, and/or actions through reflection and experiences, that the information becomes knowledge that is now their own. I like to refer to this process as "moving it from one part of the brain to another." Once it becomes their own, they can apply it to new situations. Under these circumstances, a deeper level of learning has occurred and change can occur.

So, the bottom line is when learning occurs, the brain physically changes. Zull talks about "the brain being 'plastic' meaning that the brain changes its own wiring, perhaps almost continuously. Like a piece of silly putty, the brain is molded and reshaped by the forces of life acting on it."[31] Learning physically changes the brain. Practice and emotion play a significant role in changing the brain, and hence learning. Practicing a skill engages neurons in the brain that, as a skill is done multiple times, reach out to other neurons. As these neurons are made to fire frequently, they grow and extend biochemically outwards to other neurons and create connections. The more connections that are made, the more the neuro-network expands. This represents knowledge and skill acquisition. The expansion of the networks and the connections is what is referred to as learning.[32] The construction of networks is consistent with contemporary understanding of learning in which people construct new knowledge and understandings based on what they already know and believe.[33] If learning is the result of building off of existing neuro-networks, then it would make sense to pay attention to and build off preexisting knowledge and beliefs that the learner brings to the table. Therefore, we must use strategies to access previous knowledge and build off it when attempting to help others learn something new, change someone's understanding, or take them to someplace new.

In some ways, designing learning opportunities is like building a house. First, the foundation represents the previous knowledge and experiences. As you build the house, you connect the new pieces to the foundation. A similar approach should be used when helping others learn. New learning opportunities need to start from and connect to the previous knowledge and preexisting neuro-networks in the brain, in order to maximize learning. As building proceeds, the house is constructed and the building materials are connected in many different ways from many different directions. Learning opportunities need to be designed so students can construct their knowledge from what they know and link it to as many other concepts as they can. This "scaffolding" helps students learn and perform better. These principles of learning apply equally to children and adults.[34]

As part of the scaffolding process, the more practice and repetition along with variability in the context in which practice occurs, the more connections are made in the brain. However, we need more to effectively learn. It turns out if we engage people's emotion in the process of learning, this will enhance learning. An emotional response from a person triggers the release of chemicals such as adrenalin (fight or flight), dopamine (reward), and serotonin (sleep and peace). These emotion-related chemicals enhance the connections among the neurons and responsiveness of neuron networks.[35] Therefore, if we can engage the emotions, connect with what people care about, we will enhance learning. Making this connection to a player's, student's, or employee's emotions clearly has important implications for their motivation. As part of the *Focus on Them* model, it is important we find ways to make learning, in its largest sense, intrinsically rewarding to those we are leading. Learning should feel good, provide some sense of mastery and success, and provide opportunities for the learner to work on topics and activities that naturally appeal to them, which could be defined as part of the planning with the end in mind.

Designing your pathways to your end-in-mind using activities and approaches that promote questioning, thinking, and learning from one another will build a sense of intellectual engagement and camaraderie that will have positive effects on your group's achievement. In addition, the process of interacting with other people requires a person to continually transition between being a receiver and creator of information. This transformation process promotes changes in the brain and hence learning. Helping members of a group promote the kind of intellectual camaraderie and the positive attitudes toward learning from one another builds a sense of community. This community connection can solve problems by building on each other's knowledge and skills, and move the group toward its goals more effectively. Collaboration is an important vehicle to promote the transformational process.

COLLABORATION

In its simplest form, collaboration is the act of working with another person or group of people to create, produce, or complete something. At the project level, I worked as a leader of a National Science Foundation (NSF) pilot project that involved eight teams consisting of a scientist, a K-12 educator, and an undergraduate educator-in-training (pre-service) to document the educational effectiveness of a research experience on all three parties. By involving scientists and K-12 educators in Earth systems research, we hoped to move the groups from the pre-project to a post-project situation as illustrated in Figure 13.

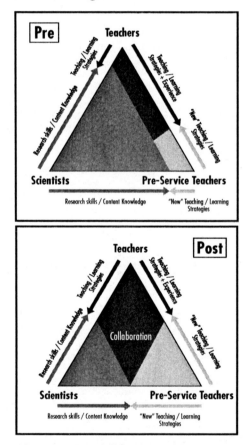

Figure 13. Pre- and post-project collaboration among scientists, teachers, and pre-service teachers in NSF pilot project. In the pre-diagram, the scientists are the ones that are in charge. In the post-diagram, the responsibilities and efforts are more equally divided. Copyright David Gosselin, Ph.D.

More explicitly, we wanted to improve the scientists' awareness of current pedagogy and classroom practices, improve K-12 teachers' understanding of actual scientific research, and expose each group to the other's unique culture.

Several of the teams were highly effective, while others struggled. The questions that emerged as we considered the effectiveness of these groups were: What were the characteristics of these highly effective teams, and what can we do to increase the probability that teams will function in this manner?

Asking these questions required me to move down a new path to find answers. At the end of this path, I found that the extent to which the individual groups effectively moved from the pre- to post-diagram was directly related to the key characteristics of effective collaboration discussed by Friend and Cook (1996)[36] and illustrated in Figure 14, and the willingness to learn. When members of a group experienced these key characteristics, one of the most fundamental outcomes was a sense that "we are all in this together," or "we sink or swim together."

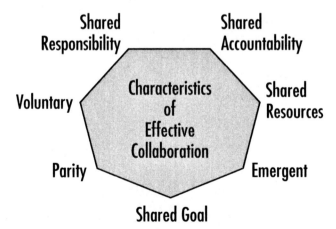

Figure 14. The key characteristics of effective collaboration.

In the context of my experiences in the NSF pilot project, here's how the elements of collaboration manifested in the effective teams.

a. Collaboration is voluntary.

There are two levels regarding the voluntary aspects of collaboration—participation and whether the participants want to use collaborative practices. Participation in this project was voluntary. The extent to which the participants wanted to use collaborative practices could explain the effectiveness of various teams. However, it should be noted we never discussed collaborative practices, so most groups functioned using their perceptions about how a team should function.

If true collaborations are to develop within teams, intrinsic motivation must be used for team members to see value in the partnership and feel that they have a clear choice to participate. Faculty can be recruited but not coerced. Pre-service teachers can be required to have inquiry experiences, but the details and commitment must be left to them; and classroom teachers must freely choose to be involved. You cannot force people to collaborate. You can throw them in a room together and tell them to be a team. Ultimately they will choose how they will work. If they have never been provided a foundation in collaborative practices, then the extent to which these practices will be used is minimized. In our case, it was the luck of the draw when we put the groups together.

b. Collaboration is based on parity.

Each member of a collaborative team must see that their contributions are equally valued, even if those contributions are drastically different. In this project, highly effective teams had members who developed and contributed unique skills for the good of the entire project. All members valued the contributions made by each member.

All team members' perspectives must be heard. Different points of view lead to better and more comprehensive outcomes. For example, the scientist was certainly the content expert, but the classroom teacher knew how the research findings ultimately had to be packaged to create curriculum, and the pre-service teacher many times became the skilled technician who held the key to good test results. The concept of being valued is critical to the success of any athletic team. Members of the most successful teams will all have a sense that their contributions to the team are important.

c. Collaboration requires a shared goal.

This characteristic emphasizes the importance of a participatory process in developing your end-in-mind. The most effective teams shared a common vision or common goals of the task and the desired outcomes. Sharing a common goal provides a strong sense of team purpose that serves as a beacon for team success. One of the biggest challenges that we created for ourselves with this project was, at the time, that we did not know how important having this shared goal would be. The driving force for establishing team makeup was the research to be accomplished. The only connection requested was that team members be willing to work together on a question established by the scientist.

From the start, this created many challenges for the teams to establish a shared goal as well as parity. We were asking these people to work together on projects based on interest in the topic. We assumed that a working relationship would form around that tie to a common interest, and by inference the team would have a shared goal. We created working teams, with a focus on the "what" these teams would do, but we invested no time or energy in "how" individuals were to work together. This was a valuable, but tough lesson to learn.

d. Collaboration is emergent.

The most successful teams spent far more time together than other project groups and, as a result, communicated with each other far more often. This time on task and open communication facilitated, and was critical to, success. The best collaborations grow as the relationships among team members grow.

As we examined the effectiveness of the teams, as defined by both products created and comments from interviews about their working relationships, we found that those more productive teams had formed working relationships that became a driving force to their work. For example, the most effective team in the project under discussion still met almost daily during the project, and the scientist and K-12 teachers continue to meet fourteen years after the project ended. They saw the results of their investment in time multiply, as each member's expertise developed. This attribute clearly suggests that short-term projects, designed for a few hours or even a couple of weeks, may fail to provide the time needed to develop effective collaboration. Newly formed teams need to spend time talking about their purpose, how they plan to work together, and what they hope to accomplish.

They also need to develop a sense of trust among team members if they are going to achieve maximum effectiveness. If they fail to develop trust, they are likely to experience difficulties later in the

process. Time with your team is critical to relationship development, which is critical to developing trust; hence, it is critical to
development of an effective collaborative team.

e. Collaboration includes shared responsibility for key decisions.

The most effective teams jointly discussed key decisions of research
design and interpretation, and every member made contributions.
On the other end of the spectrum, in the least effective teams, generally one member of the team, typically the scientist, told team
members what to do and when. This approach sabotaged the entire
collaborative process. As a result, not only did the team members
not have a shared goal, they did not have an opportunity to get
truly invested in the project, because they had nothing invested
in defining the outcomes—because they had nothing invested in
the decisions. The educators were not treated as equals and acted
accordingly. Promoting shared responsibility for key decisions can
be accomplished through consensus-based decision-making. It is
critical that the team members need to take responsibility to define
what they mean by consensus-based decision-making and how it
will be used.

f. Collaboration includes shared accountability for outcomes.

Because members of effective teams favored direct input into key
decisions, they stood ready to take full responsibility for accomplishing the needed tasks. In addition, because they established
open communication, members knew their roles and felt a sense of
responsibility to each other.

Promoting a sense of individual accountability among all team members is an important attribute for creating a shared sense of accountability, as well as shared responsibility. Individual accountability is

observed when each member of the team takes responsibility for speaking up, contributing to group discussions and decision-making, praising the contributions of others, following through on identified tasks, and reflecting on the overall functioning of the team.

g. Collaboration is based on shared resources.

Just as each member must have a sense of parity, members must feel that their contribution plays a crucial role in task accomplishment. Team members can contribute time, space, equipment, expertise, or other assets. In whatever shape or form they are contributed, the contribution of the resources should be acknowledged.

METACOGNITION FOR COLLABORATION

Metacognition is an awareness or analysis of one's own learning or thinking process. It is not a specified characteristic from Friend and Cook. It is, however, a critical but often underutilized strategy that should be integrated into collaboration. That is, during collaboration, the group should regularly reflect on the degree to which the team is adhering to its group norms and collaborative principles. Effective teams create specific times for group reflection that establish a "safe space" for group members to comment on how well collaboration is occurring.

APPLICATION – COACHING

In every sport, every player needs specific skills to be successful. Without the basic technical skills, tactics and strategies will not do you much good. In soccer, we use a training approach that applies a three-stage progression for technical skill development—fundamental stage, match-related stage, and game-related stage. You basically go from the simple to the complex, by increasing the reality of the playing environment. As the playing environment becomes more like the real game, there is a transition from individual focus to a collaboration focus as the situation becomes more like the real game. In essence, the neurons in the brain begin to connect, the networks build, so the complexity of the connections make the actions seem automatic, so to speak.

In the fundamental stage, there is no pressure from an opponent. The activities are designed to provide lots of repetition so the technique can become a skill, as evidenced by use in a game.

The match-related stage introduces some level of pressure by adding defensive players—you might play three vs. one (3 v 1), for instance. There might be time and space restrictions. Then, increase the complexity so it is more real.

The last stage is game- or match-related, where it looks like the real game. Teams have the same number of players, or even numbers in coaching vernacular. They are playing to goal. The point here is the three-stage progression is mimicking what is going on in the brain. It is also extremely important to use questions with the players about how, what, and why they do things on the field to create a reflective mentality. Engaging their brain in the process of skill development will yield long-term benefits.

APPLICATION – EDUCATION

There are numerous learning theories and instructional models. The 5E instructional model is a constructivist model.[37] It is designed to promote construction of knowledge. The concept behind the model is to begin with students' current knowledge, make connections between current knowledge and new knowledge, provide direct instruction of ideas the students would not be able to discover on their own, and provide opportunities to use and demonstrate what they know.[38]

The 5Es are engagement, exploration, explanation, elaboration, and evaluation. If we engage students in these activities, they will have a chance to use more parts of their brain and increase their level of learning. Through engagement, we connect to prior knowledge and elicit an emotional connection with the concept and content. Then, the student is provided the opportunity to explore the concepts through activities. Following exploration, we want them to explain their understanding of new concepts, processes, and skills to create conceptual clarity and cohesion. The elaboration phase activities allow students to apply concepts in contexts, and build on or extend understanding and skill. They also should challenge conceptual understanding and skills through new experiences that develop deeper and broader understanding and application. Finally, the students evaluate their knowledge, skills, and abilities, and assess their understanding and progress toward educational outcomes.

The approaches can vary, but the basic idea is to get the person to access, use, and apply what they know to new situations in order to become problem solvers. Accessing, using, and applying engages the whole brain in learning. I refer to this as moving and using data and information in different parts of the brain.

Whether you are a student, soccer player, or employee, the simple act of providing an explanation for something you are doing transforms the person from a receiver of information to a producer of information.

Throughout this 5E process, the activities should be designed to include the principles of collaboration so that people are working with one another to access previous knowledge, building new conceptual understanding and creating new ideas from these meanings, and showing how these new ideas can be applied to solving problems. When all is said and done, there should be new opportunities to generate new experiences in which they receive information and feedback on their ideas from their collaborators in learning.

APPLICATION – BUSINESS

One of the most sought-after competencies in business is the ability to work collaboratively on a team. Whether it is in the board room or trying to figure out the supply chain for a product, a large and growing number of people, processes, and places are involved and extend to global networks. Between all the processes and places are people who all seem to speak different languages—financial, legal, human resources, engineering, marketing, design, and the list goes on. The more multicultural, multilingual, multinational the business, the harder it is to exchange the knowledge necessary for timely decision-making. To translate among and between the different languages and perspectives requires the creation of an environment that uses the key characteristics of collaboration and some type of process by which people learn. Using the engagement and exploration part of the 5E model to unearth current understanding and address misconceptions and how different groups see the problem will help the group move forward effectively. This approach will take an investment of time up front, but it will get work done sooner in the long run by reducing confusion, establishing shared goals that are based on the realities that each group brings to the table, and creating new ideas that integrate in new ways the information from all groups.

We are always amazed at why people get bored at meetings and become disengaged when the meeting is designed as a one-way delivery of information. The answer is that we are not letting them use their brains. Meetings can be designed to actively engage attendees' brains through active participation. Then, they are being asked to think.

One of the beautiful things about applying collaboration and learning to get to the end in mind is that it creates the opportunity for people who have very different perspectives to share and learn from each other. Using a collaboration-based learning approach to take a group to someplace new builds a sense of community in which the sharing and learning promotes intellectual engagement and cognitive development for all parties involved. Engaging people in this approach has another significant benefit in that it builds relationships and trust that, in turn, allows for a substantial increase in value because of the additive effect of two or more brains functioning to some extent as a collective entity. This should lead to better solutions and more efficient pathways to your goals. This is consistent with the old adage that two heads are better than one when trying to solve a problem.

CHAPTER 8

How Do You Assess Success?

How do you know you have won? When the energy is coming
the other way and when your people are visibly growing
individually and as a group.

— Sir John Harvey-Jones, English businessman and author

As I have considered my role as a coach, teacher, and leader in the
context of the *Focus on Them* model, the greatest satisfaction I get
is watching people grow and come together as a group. I have also
learned another valuable lesson, and that is there is more to being
successful than the final outcome. For example, a coach's win-loss
record, a grade point average for a group of students, or an end of
year financial statement for a business.

Without question, it is more fun to win than it is lose, but if we
focus only on the outcome, we miss all the great things that are
going on in front of us on the way to the win or loss. These things
include: players being successful at something that they had been
working on for weeks; seeing one of your less gifted players strip
the ball from the best player on the other team time after time;

watching your outside back run down the sideline and get the ball from the midfielder in space and make a great cross; seeing new friendships form that you never expected; and watching boys and girls turn into young men and women, knowing that you helped them along the way.

Winning is an outcome-oriented measure similar to many others such as grades or scores on a standardized test in education, financial metrics in business, or other specific outcome-oriented goals. The problem with outcome goals is either you reach them or you don't; you succeed or fail, win or lose. In essence, you are promoting a fixed mindset mentality a la Carol Dweck, in which success is measuring up to a fixed standard.

An example of a fixed mindset focus on outcome in a business setting could be the extent to which an individual or group is valued, based on the extent to which they achieve a targeted profit margin. If they don't make it, they would be considered to be losers. Alternatively, using Dweck's growth mindset focus, the group would document improvement along the way, and if they achieve the outcome, great, but they have made progress anyway, and they are still moving forward. It is not an all or nothing approach.

Although you may be capable of more, with a fixed mindset you stop once you meet your number and, worse, you stop trying to do things differently because you are afraid of failure. Personally, I want to be interacting with a group of people who have a growth mindset. They thrive on challenge and see failure not as evidence for a lack of success but as a springboard for growth and for stretching their existing abilities. In a growth mindset, the person, group, or business recognizes that there are many factors and challenges that may influence the outcome over which they have no control, so they design their approach to focus on the processes and factors over which they do have control. They look for ways to learn and cultivate success through effort and deliberate practice, and expand their use of their qualities such as intelligence and creativity, among others.

One of the best games that I had the honor of coaching was actually a six to one loss on a beautiful, yet very windy, Saturday morning in October in Omaha, Nebraska. Reflecting back on the outcome of this game demonstrates the growth mindset in action. It was a Nebraska State Cup game against a team that went on to win the U-17 girls' state soccer title, among others. This team had at least seven NCAA Division I recruits. My team had three players who would go on to play NCAA Division III and/or NAIA soccer. We could have played this team 100 times. We would have lost 100 times. Before we went out on the field, I emphasized a quote by Michelle Akers that I had given to the team earlier in the season as part of my coaching philosophy and team operation information. Akers, arguably one of the best and most competitive players to ever play for the U.S. Women's National soccer team, stated, "My goal every game is to walk off the field (win or lose) and be able to say I did my very best and gave all I had . . . I am going to make them work for it and (they) remember playing against me."

This quote is where I want my players to be mentally, when they step on the field or the court. Win or lose, individual players and the team as a whole should strive to be remembered by the teams they play as the team that played hard and with heart, showed good sportsmanship, competed to the end, and never gave up regardless of the score. My final words for the team on that windy morning as they walked to the field were to be sure that the other team "Remembered the Rowdies."

If one was to look at the final score, it would appear as though we did not give them a very good game, but I honestly feel this talented team remembered the Rowdies. Almost as soon as the game started, we were down two-nil after the first two minutes on arguably two of the best goals I have ever seen at the club-soccer level. Some teams would have rolled over and quit. Not this team. Everyone, to a player, gave an awesome performance against a very, very good team. The Rowdies played as a unit. They played for themselves. They played for each other. When we scored in the second half, the team celebrated as though we had won the championship game. They left it all on the field for 90 minutes. They gave maximum effort that frustrated the other team to the extent that they started getting on each other. The girls recognized this and realized they had won the mental part of the contest. As a coach I could not have asked for anything more and, in fact, as a coach I should expect nothing less.

I don't think anyone can imagine how proud I was to be the Rowdies' coach on that Saturday. The team focused on what they had control over. They were winners regardless of the outcome on the scoreboard. To have measured the success of the Rowdies that day based only on the outcome-oriented measure on the score-board would not have given them credit for, nor done justice to, what they truly accomplished on that fall day. The key point here is that there is more to measuring the success and progress of individuals, your team, or business than outcome-oriented measurements.

As part of the growth mindset, your assessment systems should document success and progress in a way that can be used in a formative way to focus your reflective processes, and change what you are doing to make it better in the future. Measurement and assessment are important, as noted by Lord Kelvin in the nineteenth century, *"I often say that when you can measure what you are speaking about, and express it in numbers, you know something about it; but when you cannot measure it, when you cannot express it in numbers, your knowledge is of a meager and unsatisfactory kind."*

Measurements can be great motivators for improvement, if used appropriately. Measurement enhances the growth mindset because you are assessing the extent to which you have achieved the goals, objectives, and/or outcomes of your plan over time. You have to be able to measure something.

If you can't measure it, you have nothing to document what you achieved, you cannot manage it, and you cannot demonstrate improvement. Measurement creates feedback, which we know is the breakfast of champions.

Feedback needs to be given, as it can be used to drive the reflective process related to how to improve and do things better. As part of the feedback process, measurement provides valuable fuel to drive people, as described by Daniel Pink's three elements of motivation—mastery, autonomy, and purpose.[39]

The pursuit of mastery drives the person's "desire to get better and better at something that matters" and extends and expands their abilities. Measurement can be used to document improving mastery. Autonomy allows people to have control over what they do, how they do it, when they do it, and whom they do it with. If assessment and measurement strategies are designed in partnership with everyone involved, then a person can use their natural desire for self-direction to take control of the task they must do successfully in order for the group to be successful. Purpose relates to accomplishing something that endures at multiple levels, and measurement provides documentation of accomplishment.

Ultimately, profit may be the outcome-oriented measure for a corporation; however, focusing on achieving the specific process-oriented measures for individuals and small groups within the corporation, in the long run, will yield higher levels of performance.

Hopefully, it is clear at this point that I am a strong advocate for using an assessment system that consists of three components (see Figure 15):

1. Promotes the attributes of a growth mindset.

2. Uses both outcome- and process-oriented measures to capture a variety of attributes that document the overall success and progress of individuals and/or team.

3. Provides feedback that triggers Pink's three elements of motivation.

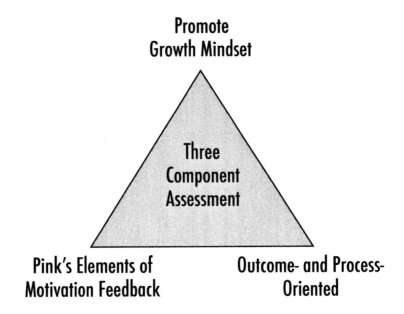

Figure 15. Three components for effective assessment, including Pink's three elements of motivation[40] and Dweck's concept of the growth mindset.[41]

Below I provide some examples.

APPLICATION – COACHING

The Positive Coaching Alliance (PCA) (http://www.positivecoach. org/) was founded in 1998 at Stanford University. The PCA emphasizes that coaches have a potentially significant influence in the lives of their athletes because many players may spend more time with their coaches than anyone else outside of their immediate family. The mission of the PCA is to develop " . . . 'Better Athletes, Better People' by working to provide all youth and high school athletes with a positive, character-building youth sports experience." One message that I find particularly compelling from the PCA is the importance of competition as they promote it, in their motto of a competitor:

- Making oneself better
- Making teammates better
- Making the game better

In his book, *The Power of Double-Goal Coaching*,[42] PCA founder Jim Thompson acknowledges that winning is important and should be a goal for every athlete. However, athletes and teams who assess themselves only on the outcomes provided on the scoreboard will have a hard time staying motivated when their opponent is superior to them and things are not going their way, or the players' skills or athleticism vary considerably within a team. Double-goal coaching provides an additional framework for motivation and assessment that employs the use of a continuous development and *mastery* approach, which leads to process-oriented development.

PCA uses the ELM Tree of Mastery for players to remember the key elements of mastery. In ELM, the E is for Effort, the L is for Learning and the M is for Mistakes are OK.

Let's go over some details: E is for Effort. The ELM Tree is clearly consistent with a growth mindset in that focus is on effort and learning, on the way to whatever outcome happens. Effort, learning, and response to making mistakes are all in the hands of the athlete. They can all be defined using both qualitative and quantitative measures as well. In fact, PCA provides a number of assessment tools for coaches and players related to ELM. At PCA, they also promote every athlete to become a Triple-Impact Competitor®— someone who strives to make themselves, their teammates, and the game better as a whole. They provide assessment worksheets to help the athletes identify strengths and weaknesses, and then promote the use of self-reflection to remind them who they are, where they are, and help them improve in all three areas as they move into the future. All of these approaches include the use of effort and stretch goals that the athlete defines, controls, and sees their progression toward achievement as they move to a new level of mastery, consistent with Pink's elements of motivation—mastery, autonomy, and purpose. Athletes experience increments of success while developing skills for their sports and other aspects of life. This approach also provides many opportunities for various types of feedback and discussion between players and coaches.

Another important constituency that coaches need feedback from is the parents, regardless of whether the players are eight-year-olds or college players. Parents should be brought into the feedback loop because they provide feedback to the players on a variety of levels, whether, as coaches, we like it or not. Creating an alliance amongst parents, players, and coaches will only make your team stronger. This goes back to knowing who you are coaching. The type and degree of the alliance will vary with the age of the player. Giving parents an opportunity for feedback will strengthen your team in the long run.

As the players get older, you want to promote the players' interpersonal skills development by advocating that each player talks with the coach directly about their concerns. However, at the same time, you need to establish a system that has rules of engagement for direct communication between the players and coaches, when appropriate.

The following is an example of an engagement approach that I use with my high school soccer team. At the preseason parent meeting, one of the themes I stress on a yearly basis is that our collective vision is to build a team that writes its own great story. The strength of the binding for this book, so to speak, is in the quantity and quality of player-coach-parent communication. Communication is a two-way street and the foundation for this street is encouraging players to "ask their questions!" We, the coaches, want to hear directly from the players (i.e., their daughters). Communicating with adults is not easy for teenagers, but it is an important life skill. We want them to take responsibility for their communication and emphasize that when they "ask their questions," they use "what" and "how" questions, and avoid those that begin in "why." For example, asking "What do I need to improve in order to get more playing time?" opens a conversation much better than "Why am I not getting playing time?" We also ask them to demand more from themselves and each other, but to do it with love.

My message to the parents is to emphasize that the coaching staff and the parents are here to support one another. We welcome discussions between parents and the coaches, however, we provide some rules of engagement. First, and foremost, if the issue is emotional or controversial, we ask the parents to invoke the 24-hour rule. We ask the parent to inform their daughter about communication with us. If the conversation is about playing time, for example, we ask that the parent and player together talk with the coach. Most often, the player knows why they are not getting the playing time that the parent perceives they should get, and this can come out during the conversation. We also understand that some topics are sensitive and require direct parent-coach communication.

Another aspect of communication, although this may seem hidden, is that we ask both the parents and players to help manage their expectations. One example of this is to minimize the comparison of their daughter to others on the team. As we tell the parents, coaches have a different perspective about individuals. Coaches know the history of the player and have seen them perform in practice. As parents, we also may be a little biased towards our own child (if you can imagine that). As a parent, your rules of engagement for communication may be different, but if your rules as a coach prohibit direct parent-coach communication—and I have experienced this—you are potentially missing a valuable alliance that would benefit the player and the team. Remember, you are all in this together.

I also strongly advocate obtaining feedback using parental assessment surveys. If you can get a representative sample of both players and parents, this provides valuable information that will help you improve the development of your team. There are many examples of these types of surveys. I have created my own to gather information about player and parental expectations for use when I start coaching a new team. For example, the PCA has partnered with "The Play Positive™ Team Parent Survey." They have developed a free, online tool for youth coaches to get feedback from parents on their child's youth sports experience. This approach provides a structured and formal process that establishes an assessment culture for coaches, administrators and organizations to foster cohesion and create a more positive playing environment. Furthermore it demonstrates a commitment to communication and feedback, and for data junkies such as myself, it can provide quantitative and qualitative data on key issues important to all parties involved, as well as to support future actions. Check out https://play-positive.libertymutual.com/programs/team-parent-survey/faq#wLk7fJg7C6DfQ1Vt.99 for more details.

APPLICATION – EDUCATION

In 2006, my colleagues and I at the University of Nebraska–Lincoln became involved in the development of online courses. These semester-long courses were designed using a modular approach. One of the big questions was, how does one document or assess learning in an environment where the instructor does not necessarily have direct oversight of the student as they work in their bedroom or apartment, miles away? We looked at a variety of traditional approaches such as quizzes and exams, etc., but none of them were very satisfactory, especially as we consider the three component assessment model that is advocated here. The outcome of our reflective deliberations was the development of what we call Content Mastery Assignments, lovingly referred to as CMAs. At the end of each course module, CMAs are used to document student learning.[43]

CMAs use an iterative grading system to help students document their mastery of and their ability to apply course content knowledge, as defined by the learning outcomes for each module. The approach promotes a growth mindset by allowing participants to revisit and resubmit their CMAs until they are satisfied with their level of mastery of the material. Their level of mastery, or performance level, is documented using an explicit and well-defined scoring rubric. There is one caveat related to submission, however: the CMA must be submitted by a specific deadline. If they choose not to submit on time they are not given the opportunity to resubmit. CMAs provide students varying degrees of autonomy over what they do and how they do it. Students can be creative by using the format of their choice for submission that includes, but is not limited to: essays, annotated PowerPoint and Prezi presentations, scrapbooks, videos, and newspaper article formats.

Although we do not explicitly teach process-oriented metacognitive skills (planning, monitoring, and evaluating), CMAs provide an opportunity for students to take control; become more confident, independent, and reflective learner; and employ higher-order cognitive learning skills. Through CMAs, students indirectly use the basic elements of metacognition to achieve the cognitive purpose of learning module-specific concepts. According to Livingston (1997),[44] cognitive (i.e., thinking and learning) and metacognitive strategies are closely intertwined and dependent upon each other. CMAs promote the use of learner-based reflection that available research indicates is effective and improves the learning outcomes of students in a variety of learning environments.[45] From my perspective, CMAs assess improvement and are both outcome- and process-oriented measures. They use Pink's elements of motivational feedback and promote the growth mindset in that the individual can strive for excellence and be the best they can be at that particular point in time.

APPLICATION – BUSINESS

Recently, I was introduced to the Balanced Scorecard system for business that incorporates, to varying degrees, the three components of assessment previously highlighted in Figure 15.

In a 1992 Harvard Business Review article, Drs. Robert Kaplan (Harvard Business School) and David Norton introduced the

Balanced Scorecard.[46] The two basic premises that underlie the Balanced Scorecard are:

1. To effectively improve and manage, you need to measure it.

2. Measurement motivates (as we have seen, from both educational and coaching perspectives).

From what I have learned, the Balanced Scorecard approach is used to expand from business and industrial use into government and nonprofit organizations. This approach aligns business activities with the vision and strategy of the organization through improvement of internal and external communications. The approach also uses holistic monitoring of organizational performance that goes above and beyond financial metrics.

Kaplan and Norton[47] advocate that if companies are to improve their outcome-oriented financial metrics, they need to manage and measure nonfinancial metrics, some of which are very much process-oriented metrics, related to three perspectives—customer, internal process, and learning and growth. In a working paper from the Harvard Business School (#10-074), Kaplan points out that the Balanced Scorecard is not the first to advocate that nonfinancial measures be used to motivate, measure, and evaluate company performance. R. Lewis in a 1950s case study[48] of General Electric indicated that divisional performance was being measured by one financial and seven nonfinancial metrics, which included such things as productivity and leadership; responsibility to shareholders, vendors, dealers, distributors, and communities; personnel development; and employee attitudes. It is beyond the scope of this book to go further into the details of the Balanced Scorecard approach. For more details and resources related to the use and implementation of the Balanced Scorecard, see http://balancedscorecard.org/.

The takeaway message is that effective assessment in coaching, education, and business may call the components something different, but they all promote the attributes of a growth mindset; they use both outcome- and process-oriented measures to capture a variety of attributes that document the overall success and progress of individuals and/or team; and they provide feedback that triggers Pink's three elements of motivation.

CHAPTER 9

Communication: The Foundation for Changing Mindsets

The basic building block of good communication is the feeling that every human being is unique and of value.

— Unknown

To effectively communicate, we must realize that we're all different in the way we perceive the work and use this understanding as a guide to our communication with others.

— Tony Robbins, American Motivational Speaker

The three most important words that are fundamental to the successful use of the model espoused throughout this book are Communication, Communication, and Communication. The ability to communicate is THE most important life skill that coaches, teachers, and leaders of employees need to develop. Like any other skill, it takes practice. The successful implementation of any of the components of this model in any organization, whether it be a soccer team, a classroom, or a business, will require the implementor to have good communication skills.

So what does it mean to have good communication skills? You would think that the answer to the question would be fairly simple. However, the phrase 'good communication skills' has become so cliché, overused, and broad, it's hard to know what it really means. So let's set up a common frame of reference.

If you have good communication skills, you have the ability to convey information to people clearly, simply, and efficiently so that things are understood and things get done. There are four basic categories of communication:

1. Spoken or verbal communication including face-to-face, telephone, radio, or television and other media.

2. Nonverbal communication including body language, gestures, how we dress or act.

3. Written communication including letters, emails, text messages, books, magazines, and web-based media.

4. Visuals including graphics, charts, maps, and other visual representations.

Regardless of the category, communication is about sending and receiving information clearly. It is not only about what the sender of the information does. It is also about what the receiver does with it and about being able to read your audience. A person can have the best communication skills in the world, but they need to be in an environment where they are comfortable using their skill sets.

CREATE AN ENVIRONMENT FOR COMMUNICATION

One of the hardest things for players, students, and employees to do is to communicate with the people whom they perceive to be

in a position of authority. Growing up, I experienced this firsthand
going to a military high school. Most of the experiences I had communicating with authority figures were usually one way, i.e., parent
to child, teacher to student, coach to player, manager to employee,
administrator to teacher. Although there are generational differences and other reasons that people have trouble communicating
with authority figures, the one-way direction of information flow
still contributes to the challenge. In the case where authority figures
create opportunities for two-way communication, negative body
language, the lack of acknowledgment of ideas, or failure to follow
through on suggestions, among other things, discourages effective
communication. Ineffective communication does not inspire trust.
Patrick Lencioni, in his book *The Five Dysfunctions of a Team: A
Leadership Fable*,[49] describes this as one of the most fundamental
problems for most teams.

If you cannot establish trust among and between team members
and the leaders, the team will be dysfunctional. It is therefore im-
perative to create an environment that promotes communication.

Over the course of my career, I was very fortunate to have had
managers and supervisors who treated those in their charge with
respect, courtesy, and professionalism. They engaged us in the processes involved in the operation. They built trust. For five and half
years as a produce clerk during high school and college, the store
managers where I worked encouraged us to bring them our ideas.
Some were used. Some were not, but, in either case, we were lis-
tened to and received feedback on our ideas. As a graduate student,
my dissertation advisor included all his students in weekly meetings
with other academic professionals and staff. We were treated like

professionals. We were kept informed and given responsibilities for the operation of various lab spaces. We were asked to actively contribute ideas to project discussions. Relationships were developed through which our strengths and weaknesses were exposed. When looking at the characteristics of collaboration, all of them were involved in both of these professional settings and as a result, trust was created amongst the members of the team. Without relationships and trust, a team is a team in name only.

My experiences in the two settings above, along with the pursuit of professional development opportunities, provided me with the foundation, i.e., models that I could build into my own approach and use with my students, my players, and, for that matter, others with whom I work. My personal goal is to encourage my players, students, and employees, my teams, to "ask their questions." From my perspective, there is no such thing as a stupid question unless you keep asking the same question over and over again and keep getting the same answer. Only then does the question become "stupid." I want the members of my teams to trust me enough to come and ask me why I am doing something the way I do it. There is usually a method to my madness and I am willing to share it with them, so I want them to feel free to ask me. I encourage them to ask how or what they can do to improve.

Asking their questions, however, is really hard for some because of a lack of opportunity to practice in the past. Along with encouraging them to ask their questions, I do my best to respond to them, both verbally and nonverbally, in a respectful and empathetic manner. I try to follow the advice from Daniel Pink and use language that is not commanding or appears to be controlling.

Instead of saying you "need to" or "have to" or "should," I try approaching it by saying, "consider" or "think about." It is a challenge to avoid using the controlling language, but in the long run it will help open channels of communication that promote interaction and engagement.

Promoting an environment where questions and inquiry are valued is not the only way to create an environment that promotes communication. Coaches, teachers, and business leaders have other great opportunities to model positive and respectful communication that will lead to the building of trust. One of these opportunities to model is through the process of providing feedback. The quote "Feedback is the breakfast of champions," often attributed to Ken Blanchard,[50] an author, management expert, and business consultant, emphasizes the importance of feedback to individual and organizational success. At the individual level, Daniel Pink, in his book *Drive*,[51] indicates that an essential ingredient to achieving mastery is getting feedback on how one is doing. However, feedback only becomes valuable when a person responds to and operationalizes it so they can improve and adjust their plans, strategies, and approaches to increase the probability of success.

FEEDBACK

Feedback can come in many shapes and forms over many different time scales—from an on-field correction during a training session by a soccer coach, to the assessment of an assignment by a teacher, to the annual performance review by a supervisor. Effective feedback, regardless of the forum for its implementation, has some common elements. First, recognize the things someone does well. When you see the type of behavior, product, etc., that you are looking for, tell them. If you identify it and tell them, you have provided positive reinforcement. You will see it again. This type of feedback will motivate them and move them towards continued improvement. This should be a goal. Be liberal with your praise. The feedback may be a simple thank you for something a person has done. It may be sending an employee a note of congratulations for something they have accomplished. Make it a point to find people doing things well.

As a supervisor who lives in a world where feedback is required only once a year as part of an annual performance review, it is strongly encouraged that you find a mechanism for providing feedback in a more timely and meaningful fashion. If you consider the analogy of your employee being like a professional athlete, a professional athlete cannot improve without regular feedback. Feedback on an annual basis to a professional athlete would not move them forward at a rate that could continue to be successful. Why should the professionals you supervise be left without feedback for a year?

There are two caveats here to keep in mind when thinking about the process of feedback. Feedback needs to be specific, accurate, and sincere. It should also focus on performance in order to promote the growth mindset as advocated by Carol Dweck in her work on mindsets. In the context of specificity, if you tell someone that they are doing a "good job" continuously, the feedback starts to mean nothing. For example, telling a young soccer player that they are doing a good job every time they touch the ball makes the feedback meaningless as time goes on. It is not specific, it is not accurate, and after a while, it may not really be sincere. As a result, the player will become numb to the feedback. They will not be able to use the feedback to support their improvement. Focus on a specific technique that they have successfully completed in a game for the first time, instead. I am sure everyone could come up with similar educational and business scenarios where specific, accurate, and sincere feedback would be useful.

As far as a focus on performance, Dweck's research supports the approach that we want to most definitely recognize people for their accomplishment, but do it in the context of the process by which they achieved it, instead of the outcome. For example, instead of congratulating a student for the A on their paper, specifically acknowledge the time and effort they invested and the strategies that they used to achieve the outcome. This will create a growth mindset which is the mindset that I want my players, students, and employees to have.

Feedback is not only about providing feedback that acknowledges positive behaviors, outcomes, contributions, etc., it is also about improving performance by correcting errors. An effective approach to this is to use what is referred to as a *feedback sandwich*. The feedback sandwich consists of three fundamental components: Identify the Positive; Coach for Correction; Encourage Positive Future Outlook.

Identify the Positive—find something significant that the individual did. Praise them for their strengths and areas of performance that met your expectations. This component helps the person become more open and responsive to the feedback that you are about to give them. For example, on an assignment, a student used a very creative approach to present the desired content, yet they are missing some critical definitions . . . you might start off by saying, *"I really appreciate the creativity you have put into this. I really like the way you have used the images to illustrate the concept."*

Coaching for Correction—you now have their attention and they are in a receptive frame of mind. Now is the time to coach and to facilitate new learning. Tell them about the behavior or performance that you observed and how it differed from the expectations. Then show and be specific as to what they need to do to improve what they have done. Be direct and firm, but never angry, never demeaning, never sarcastic. You want to keep the channels of communication open. So to continue with the example above: *"To improve your presentation and to take advantage of your images, it would be useful to add some specific definitions for concepts you are illustrating so the audience knows specifically what you are trying to communicate."*

Encourage Positive Future Outlook—inevitably your feedback probably will cause some mental deflation so it is a good idea to project a positive outcome on the situation. Start by restating the positive phrase with which you began, outline the ways to improve, and highlight how the combination will lead to even better results. *"Please continue to use your creative approach and by adding the details that explicitly define the content, you will have created an excellent piece of informational material that will serve you well in the future."* There are many nuances to using the feedback sandwich—keep your language neutral; it is about the performance, not the person; get don't, but, and should out of your vocabulary; be timely, etc. A quick web search will yield all types of helpful hints to address these nuances. It does take practice, but the sooner you start the better you will be.

ESTABLISH EXPECTATIONS

Another attribute for creating an environment for communication is to establish an expectation of positive communication and interaction among members of your team. We have a tendency to see the things that went wrong rather than what went right. We definitely need to identify areas for improvement but we need to expect a culture of positive communication from those we lead, to improve in the future. Establishing a positive communication environment also is promoted through accepting the differences that people have in their behavioral and motivational styles, and learning how to modify our approaches accordingly.

Positive communication is not as simple as it sounds. It takes practice. It requires everyone on the team to adapt to the differences in behavioral and motivational styles that exist between us and the other members of the team.

It is also important to set expectations with regard to communication in the context of openness, professionalism, and respect. I try to communicate what they can expect from me and, in turn, I also communicate what I expect from them. I share my coaching, educational, and/or management philosophy with my players, students, and/or employees. Sharing this with them gives them a better sense for who I am, which helps in the development of trust. For my soccer players and students, I want them to tell me when they are going to miss practice or class. Communication needs to be more than just a text that says, "I will not be at practice (or class)." I want them to tell me why. In the business environment, similar expectations should be established as well.

As part of an open communication policy, I strongly advocate that everyone use the "24-hour rule." This rule is particularly important when stress and emotions are involved. The purpose of this rule is to delay your communication until you have calmed down, to reduce the chance for an emotional overreaction, and increase the opportunity to more rationally think about the situation. Waiting 24 hours will increase the probability that you can more clearly communicate your issue with a cool head.

We have all received troubling and even nasty emails from people regarding our decisions. I once received a message from a father who basically told me that my coaching decisions had lost the game for our team that afternoon. When I received this message, I was not too happy and I am sure I gnashed my teeth in frustration. Interestingly, he had not even attended the game and his analysis was based on information from his daughter, who, by the way, had no idea that he was communicating with me, nor does she to this day. I cannot tell you how I wanted to reply back and tell him he had a lot of nerve, among other things. However, I invoked my own rule and I sent him a reply back the next day. It turns out that even prior to receiving his analysis, I had replayed and reflected on the entire game in my head more than once, as we coaches often do, and recognized that I had goofed. As part of my reply, I did acknowledge that my substitution decisions at the end of the game likely contributed to our loss. I never indicated how annoyed I was that a person who was not at the game provided a critical analysis. Instead, I encouraged him in the future to have his daughter come to talk to me directly about her concerns.

There was no question that I learned a lot from that game. Using the 24-hour rule helped keep the peace in the family, so to speak. It minimized the opportunity for the situation to escalate to the point where it had a negative impact on the team.

NONVERBAL LANGUAGE

There are many old sayings that come to mind when one considers the importance of nonverbal communication. These old sayings include "your actions speak louder than your words" or "a picture is worth a thousand words." The list could go on. These old sayings reflect what has been documented in a variety of studies. One of the most often cited percentages is that 93% of communication is nonverbal and 7% is verbal, which comes from a 1972 work by Dr. Albert Mehrabian in his book *Silent Messages*.[52]

Work by researchers at the Nonverbal Group (http://www.nonverbalgroup.com/) indicate that the amount of nonverbal communication varies between 60 and 90 percent on a daily basis. Regardless of what the actual numbers are, nonverbal communication can provide a person with lots of information, some of which may be unintended. Sometimes this nonverbal language communicates a different message than our spoken word. Body movements are subtle, often simple. Movements, gestures, or facial expressions are signs and signals that give away how you really may be feeling. The way we talk, walk, sit, and stand provides a lot of information that can have an important effect on how others act and react towards us.

A story will help illustrate the importance of nonverbal communication and its impact on the environment of communication. As a soccer coach, it took me awhile to realize how my body language was impacting the performance of my team, especially in the early parts of the game. Over the course of several seasons, I began to notice a pattern. If I was sitting in a chair on the sideline during the first part of the game, my team seemed to start faster and stronger. When I was not sitting, my nonverbal body language apparently made me an open book as to how I was feeling. At times, my body language painted a picture of frustration to the young ladies I was coaching. When they picked up on my frustration, they began to stress and it was reflected in a diminished quality of their play.

It is amazing the impact that a simple drop of the head after someone misses a shot on goal can have on the psyche of the player—regardless of the fact that I would give the player a positive verbal phrase such as "get the next one" or "good choice." The verbal signals were not consistent with what I was nonverbally communicating. It took me awhile but I finally started sitting in a chair on the sidelines, especially in the early stages of the game, as my players would pick up on body language and it impacted the way they played.

Similarly, nonverbal language can manifest in the classroom or the boardroom. Breathing rate, perspiration, eye movement and contact, body movements and gestures (facial expressions, legs, arms, hands, head, and torso), posture, muscle tension, tone of voice, rate of speech, and pitch of the voice all add to the words being used. When implementing our plans, we may not be able to eliminate what might be interpreted as negative body language, but if you are more aware of it, you may be able to minimize it. This puts you in a better position to communicate effectively with those whom you coach, teach, or lead, and, in turn, will allow you to question the individuals about their signals and get to know them better.

AGE-APPROPRIATENESS

Earlier in the book, I addressed the importance of generational differences and age-related differences between and among you and your players, students, and employees. It is important to remember these differences when communicating with them. There are fundamental differences between communicating with a group of adults and a group of eight-year-olds. This seems rather obvious, but I think you would be surprised how often as a coach, educator, or employer you will use words that your players have never heard before, even when talking to college-age students. You may find yourself talking about concepts that your players may not have the ability to understand because of their age and cognitive development.

For the first time, four generations of employees are simultaneously in the workplace. This creates some interesting communication challenges. I am sure you have also experienced referring to a TV show or a song from the 1970s, and were amazed that your players and students, who were born in the late 1990s or early 2000s, have never heard of them. We think we are providing a relevant story, when in reality, we missed the mark by twenty years. There are also differences in what is appropriate—old-school formality of using company letterhead vs. a quick email to a client using texting-based abbreviations. Being aware of the differences is a place to start. Talking about the differences and expectations is even better for reducing generation-related communication challenges.

GENDER-RELATED ISSUES

In his eye-opening, bestselling book, *Men Are from Mars, Women Are from Venus*, John Gray emphasizes the importance of understanding the communication style and emotional needs of men and women in the context of improving relationships between the two genders. According to John Medina in *Brain Rules*,[53] there are structural and biochemical differences between the brains of men and women that may contribute to how the genders emotionally respond to various situations, how they communicate, and how they develop relationships.

A growing body of research documents the influence that the environment has on men's and women's self-perception and perception of the other gender. It is not uncommon that the behaviors of parents and other adults towards boys and girls influence their behaviors. In general, boys are encouraged to be independent and are played with more roughly, whereas many more limits are placed on the acceptable behavior for girls, and they are treated more delicately and gently.

As pointed out in the book, *The Gendered Society*,[54] Kimmel (2000) indicates the seeds of gender differences are first established in the family. This is where boys and girls are first exposed to the meaning of being a man or women or boy or girl. Although they may not realize it, parents possess a set of gender-specific ideas of what their children need and have certain beliefs about what girls and boys should be like at various ages. Lott[55] argues that toys for girls encourage dependency on others, while toys for boys stress independence and problem solving. Girls are rewarded for their looks and being attractive, while boys are rewarded for their physical performance and for being active. Girls are taught to capitalize on their external features and seek approval from others, whereas boys discover that athletic ability and individual performance are important to succeed as a male.

The answer regarding the nature vs. nurture question has not been answered. However, we must acknowledge that there are differences and admit that "You and me, we come from different worlds," as Hootie and the Blowfish advocate in one of their more famous hits, "Only Wanna Be With You." There is nothing wrong with either of these two worlds, it is just that they are different and they bring different perspectives and approaches to the table that are very important to consider.

From my own experience, I am glad that I have accepted the reality that there are inherent challenges in communicating with and understanding what motivates female athletes. I have learned that first and foremost, I am coaching an athlete and not the gender in the context of the skills, knowledge of the game, mental abilities, and fitness, among others. I hope I have learned to be cognizant of my female athletes' feelings and how important it is to develop relationships with them. One mistake I have seen a number of male coaches make, and which is emphasized as a huge mistake by Anson Dorrance,[56] is trying to motivate girls and women with the intensity of their own personalities.

As males, we have all experienced aggressive, loud, in-your-face motivational exhortations from our coaches or constant yelling that consistently told us what we have done wrong. Although this approach is not advocated for either male or female athletes, male athletes will respond to this type of motivational strategy. This, in turn, leads to the assumption that if it worked for me it will work for them (note: recall the section about assumptions can kill). Unfortunately, this communication style is generally counterproductive when it comes to female athletes. Because female athletes are more relationship-oriented, this motivational approach may be interpreted as a personal attack and female athletes will feel that their relationship with the coach has been affected by their play on the field. This feeling eventually evolves into the female athletes developing a sense that there is a personal distance between themselves and their coach, because of their apparent athletic failure. If this situation is not remedied, I have seen a coach's ability to lead some female athletes reduced. According to Dorrance, "It's crucial when you are coaching women to use the correct tone and body language to communicate, or at least have some sort of positive approach even if you are being critical."[57] Silby and Smith (2000) highlight this perspective further, "Coaches, whether male or female, should be aware that female athletes . . . want to develop personal relationships with them and prefer coaches who communicate openly and are empathetic. Female athletes value friendship and like to focus on team unity. . . . They place a high value on personal improvement and prefer not to have their confidence attacked."[58]

Although it is beyond the scope of this book to discuss all of the factors that influence gender differences, it should be apparent that there are inherent psychological differences between males and females that will influence communication between genders. This seems rather obvious, but think about your personal relationships with your significant other or your children, and the communication challenges that you may have. Now take that into a coaching, education, or business environment where you do not have the same level of strengths in your relationship. Your ability to implement the approaches described here depends on being able to address these gender differences. And, your sensitivity to these and other personality differences will impact your ability to create an environment where communication, communication, communication can flourish.

CHAPTER 10

Bring It All Together:
Take on New Challenges

Coming together is a beginning, staying together is progress,
and working together is success.

— Henry Ford

Intellectual growth should commence at birth and cease only at death.

— Albert Einstein

In every facet of our lives, we see leadership in action in work and play, over different time scales from minutes to years, and from one-on-one interactions in the case of "lollipop moments" to presidents leading millions. Given that there are so many ways and so many scales in which leadership manifests itself, it is no wonder there is a plethora of ideas and terminology related to leadership definitions, descriptions, theories, models, and styles. As is the case with leadership, coaching and teaching are similar because they can be defined in a variety of ways, over a variety of scales, and described by many theories, models, and styles.

Although there is a range of definitions, models, and theories, coaching, teaching, and leading all have one common attribute: they all involve processes that take a person or group of people to someplace new and move people forward. These processes all involve change. Any time change occurs, some level of learning is involved. Therefore coaching, teaching, and leading are all about learning.

Whether they realize it or not, the most effective coaches, teachers, and leaders not only use methods and strategies that most effectively engage the brains of the people involved, but they also continually reflect, ask questions, and look for ways to improve what they do.

As we approach the end of this book, I would like you to continue to reflect, ask questions, and look for ways that the concepts presented here will help improve what you do. More specifically, I would like you to address one or more of the following challenges.

CHALLENGE 1. TEST THE HYPOTHESIS

The hypothesis proposed at the beginning of this book is that using the five questions summarized in Figure 3 will increase your effectiveness as a leader, teacher, or coach. Since I began conceptualizing this book, I have invested a considerable amount of time applying the five questions to a range of challenging coaching, teaching, and leadership situations that I have recently encountered. My approach has been to examine these situations in the context of the five questions.

- Who am I as a leader, coach, or educator?

- Who am I leading—students, players, employers, etc.?

- Where do I want to lead them? Am I planning with the end in mind?

- How do I get them there?

- How do we know when we get there?

Then ask yourself how could this situation be improved if the leader, coach, or teacher would have answered one or all of these questions prior to or during the situation? This could be a situation that you were directly involved in, or someone that you know.

CHALLENGE 2. LEARN MORE ABOUT YOURSELF

Consider the hours that you spend with your players, students, and employees and the influence that you have on them. One of the current catch phrases in the business world is "adapt for success." However, to adapt you need to know where you are starting from and what you might be adapting to. Some things to know about yourself might include your behavioral style, motivational drivers, and emotional intelligences, among others. For example, my behavioral (coordinator) and primary motivational (theoretical) tendencies may create some potential challenges that I will need to address through adaptation. Specifically as a coordinator, I need to be more conscious about being more direct and open in my communication with students who have the behavioral characteristics of persuaders. They will also need to recognize that they will need to follow through with what they say they are going to do. From the motivational side of things, with my high theoretical tendencies, I need to recognize that students who have social motivational tendencies may see me as callous and uncaring.

There are a variety of instruments that can be used to gather these types of data. None of these instruments are perfect by any means, but they do provide valuable information about who you are and who you are not. Furthermore, the outcomes from these instruments are not intended to be used as excuses. They are to be used as objective tools that can open channels of communication between and amongst people.

Assessments help us better understand what motivates us and explore our self-perception. Most of the literature on leadership supports the contention that knowing yourself increases your ability to be an effective leader.

CHALLENGE 3. ARTICULATE YOUR PHILOSOPHY

I strongly encourage you to reflect and articulate your coaching, teaching, or leadership philosophy. When I say articulate, I mean write it down and then tell someone about it. You will be amazed what a clarifying experience it can be. I guess one could say that this book is an extended articulation of my attempt to integrate my leadership, educational, and coaching philosophies. Your process of reflection and articulation will be very different than mine, but it will be equally as valuable. Being able to articulate your philosophy to others will help you establish communication and understanding during your interactions with them.

As you reflect on your philosophy, you may want to consider some of the following questions:

- Why do I coach?
- Why do I teach?
- What is success?
- What is appropriate behavior for me as a leader?
- Am I being a role model for my players, students, or employees?

Answers to these questions describe the foundation of our teaching, coaching, and leadership philosophies. You may also find yourself feeling overwhelmed, considering the responsibility and the potential impact that you have on those you coach, teach, or employ. These impacts you have can be positive or negative, depending on many factors. If you think back about a teacher, coach, or boss who had a major positive impact on you, I suspect one of the key remembrances is how they cared about you. Articulating your philosophy to yourself and then to others is the foundation for showing you care.

CHALLENGE 4. LEARN MORE ABOUT WHOM YOU ARE LEADING, TEACHING, AND COACHING

Although this is the fourth challenge, it is probably the most fundamental one related to the *Focus on Them* theme of this book. As part of this entire journey going to someplace new, I challenge you to do two things:

1. Consistently ask the question, who am I leading, coaching, and/or educating?

2. Leave your assumptions at the door.

Throughout this book, a variety of approaches and range of informational resources have been suggested. These are places to start. I encourage you to explore other resources. They all have value. However, there is not a one-size-fits-all answer to the questions. Every person and group you teach, coach, or lead will be different. To make assumptions about the characteristics and motivations of individuals and groups can lead you down a very slippery slope. Accept the fact that they are not you, and learn who they really are. No matter how hard you try, you will still catch yourself making assumptions, but hopefully not as often. Keep practicing to leave assumptions at the door because practice makes perfect.

In the context of building any team or coherent group, it takes more than just calling yourself a team. Building a team takes time and the development of trust. "Trust lies at the heart of a functioning, cohesive team . . . trust is the confidence among team members that their peers' (and their leader's) intentions are good and there is no reason to be protective or careful around the group. In essence, teammates (and their leaders) must get comfortable being vulnerable with one another."[59] Among other things, developing trust requires a deep understanding of the unique characteristics of the team members. The extent to which you can learn about the individuals and groups will be a function of the time you have to engage with them and the size of the group. I refer you to Lencioni, among others, for specific suggestions and activities, including the use of behavior assessments to learn about your "team members."

Investing time in learning about others while at the same time learning about yourself is critical to the development of your team. It is not easy. It will take time. It will be worth it.

CHALLENGE 5. BECOME A REFLECTIVE, METACOGNITIVE PRACTITIONER

Earlier in the book, the importance of using a variety of approaches for assessment was emphasized. Assessment provides the foundation for feedback, which is the breakfast of champions. From my perspective, assessment is valuable only if it is used to improve what you are doing, and to inform the questions that you are asking. To improve and inform, you need to reflect on how, what, and why you are doing what you are doing. Continuously asking questions in the context of improving what you are doing will make you a reflective practitioner. Taking reflection to a more personal level, improving your awareness or analysis of your own learning and thinking processes and the extent to which you adhere to the norms and principles that you have articulated in your coaching, learning, and/or leadership philosophy, is practicing the skill of metacognition. I encourage you to become a reflective and meta-cognitive practitioner.

CHALLENGE 6. IMPROVE THE ENVIRONMENT FOR COMMUNICATION

The ability to communicate is THE most important life skill that coaches, teachers, and leaders of employees need to develop. Like any other skill, it takes practice. The successful implementation of any of the components of the approach advocated in this book for use in any organization, whether it be a soccer team, a classroom, or a business, will require the implementor to have good communication skills. Many resources can be consulted to improve your skills. Without doubt, improving your communication skills will help improve your communication environment.

In addition to skills and other attributes outlined in the previous chapter on communication, I would strongly endorse two actions that will further enhance your communication environment.

First: encourage questions and dialogue. One of things that I have noticed among players, students, and employees, is their reticence, or even fear, to ask questions. This reticence and fear has resulted from a variety of circumstances and experiences. If questions are not asked, especially as they relate to how things can be done better, progress in any organization will be inhibited. Putting the brains of all your team members to work can only lead to greater success. My personal goal is to encourage my players, students, and employees (my teams) to "ask their questions." There is usually a method to my madness and I am happy to share that with the groups. There are times when I do not know the answer, and these times open up new pathways to explore with others to find the answer. If you encourage questions, be sure you listen authentically to them—listen respectfully, respect their values and beliefs, and present genuine concern for their thoughts and ideas. Listen to them with empathy and be sure to listen and respond to the question in a respectful way. Your responses will lead to more questions, but more importantly, the quality of the questions will improve. From my perspective, there is no such thing as a stupid question unless the same question is asked over and over again and the same answer is given. Take the challenge to ask those you lead to ask their questions.

Second: show that you care. If you think back to those people you consider to be the best coach, teacher, or leader you have had, I am fairly confident that you got the sense that they cared about you. The way in which they gave you that sense of being cared about likely varied from one situation to another. Showing you care will contribute to development of an environment of trust that will lead to more open communication and the progress each individual and your organization will make as a whole. Regardless of how you do it, take the challenge to let them know you care!

As I reflect back on my coaching, educating, and leadership journey so far, I consider all the players, students, and employees, and I sometimes wonder if it is all worth it. Then, like me, you may get a letter or a note from a former player such as the one from Anna, and you get a sense of the impact that you have had. However, for me it was getting a letter like the following one from my sixteen-year-old daughter, who had experienced more than her fair share of my leadership experiments, challenged me many times along the way, and was an intimate part of my leadership journey, it hit home and I realized that I had really done "something good," and she really knows I care.

Dear Dad,

I would like to say THANK YOU, THANK YOU, THANK YOU!!!! . . . I know I don't show my appreciation for you that much, but I am grateful for everything you do for me.

First of all, I would like to thank you for being my coach. I know sometimes you get frustrated with us, especially me. But I am really glad that you can get through the troubles and keep going. It means a lot that you have stuck with me and worked with me so patiently and consistently. I am really happy that you are willing to spend your time working with me so I can reach the goals I want to reach. The reason why I have succeeded in soccer is because of you. Your willingness to go to Square D to practice my shot and time my 120s means the world to me. Your small sacrifices have made me the player I am today.

Last year at the beginning of the soccer season, (Coach) Ekeler told us to dedicate our season to one person. He wanted us to play for someone rather than ourselves. I took this challenge and dedicated my season to you. When we were doing the conditionings after practice, and I didn't want to go anymore, I thought of you and that gave me the determination to keep going. Your encouraging words would come to my head, "Megan, you can do anything you set your mind to. I believe you can do anything." These hopeful words would give me the courage to push through one more set. When I scored my first varsity goal, I thought of you. "I hope my dad saw that one, because that's what we've been working on to improve." Every moment I played, you were in the back of my head pushing me to go that extra set, to set me apart from the rest.

Finally, I would like to clear up a misconception you probably have. I really, really, really like you coaching me. Although I put up that hard shell against you, I truthfully value every moment I have with you coaching me. Like I said before, I am in the place I'm at with soccer because of you. I am grateful for everything you do and never let anything I say or do change that truth in your mind. So, pretty much what I want to say is YOU ARE THE GREATEST!!!!!

Love,

Megan

ACKNOWLEDGMENTS

Over the years, I have had the pleasure to learn from and collaborate with a large number of talented, insightful, intelligent, and caring people. Although this writing project started almost a year ago, the story told here is the culmination of my learning over many years from many people—colleagues, students, players. Because learning never ends, my intent is to add to these experiences using www. DaveGosselinPhd.com as I continue to progress along my leadership journey.

This book is a culmination of a variety of paths converging that started in very different places. One of these paths started with a simple question from my daughter, "Will you coach my soccer team?" A second path started with the statement, "Earth science is dead in Nebraska." A third path started with a question, "How can I become a better leader?" These three paths led to a variety of other paths that allowed me to learn from and be mentored by some great people—Doug Williamson, Ron Bonnstetter, and Mark Kuzila. Doug led me down the coaching path to the many facets of educational and leadership programs offered by the National Soccer Coaches Association of America (NSCAA). Ron challenged me to rethink my educational philosophy, helped me focus on the needs of those I was trying to educate and coach, as well as continually reminding me of the importance of knowing self. Mark challenged me daily, many times over coffee, to step back, take a breath, and focus on what is important when leading, educating, and coaching, the THEM emphasized throughout this book. Another important mentor from my younger days, Bob Collopy, modeled the importance of showing you care as an educator, which at the time I really needed, and still influences me to this day. I greatly appreciate the support from Bill Bonnstetter and his team at TTI Success Insights for providing me with the opportunity to apply their industry-leading tools to students and players. Moreover, TTI has allowed me to use many of their diagrams in this book and participate in the TTI annual conference, where I have seen the application of their tools and met some fascinating people. The relationship with the Bonnstetter brothers has introduced me to some inspirational and very helpful people, including Ron Price, who provided insightful feedback on this book, and Whit Mitchell. Conversations with both Ron and Whit strongly influenced my decision to move forward on this project.

Many others over the years have led me to different resources and allowed me to participate in leadership training opportunities as well as practice leadership in a range of venues. I greatly appreciate the opportunities that have been provided by the University of Nebraska–Lincoln. The feedback on this book from Mike Tobias, Megan Gosselin, Stephanie Emodi, Doug Williamson, Ron Bonnstetter, and Ron Price was insightful and challenged me. Your contributions and the investment of your time in this project are greatly appreciated. Over the years, I have had great students to work with, especially in the Environmental Studies program. I have learned a lot from you. My coaching path has given me the opportunity to interact with a large number of players and parents. All of you have positively contributed in some way, shape, or form to my journey. Thank you.

The patience, commitment, encouragement, and support of my publishing team at Aloha Publishing including Maryanna Young, Hannah Cross, and Jennifer Regner have contributed immensely to the book. I was not too sure what I was getting into when this project started, but they helped me navigate the process and overall have been a great group with which to collaborate.

Last, but certainly not least, I am extremely thankful for my wife, Beth, who has been a very supportive partner throughout my journey. She has been there to keep me on track and help me keep my focus on what is important. My daughter Megan had the opportunity to experience many of my leadership and coaching experiments. She challenged me at times and this led me to making things better. Her input and support has been invaluable. My oldest daughter, Amy, got me going down the coaching path and for that I am grateful. It has taken me to places I never would have gone.

ABOUT THE AUTHOR

Dave Gosselin believes we all have the capacity to be leaders and change someone's life. Over the past 30 years, he has developed a passion for coaching, educating, and modeling leadership for young people. His own journey has made it clear that a mindset change to the *Focus on Them* message will help us become more effective coaches, leaders, or educators. Dave has coached soccer for more than nineteen years at the youth, high school, and college level, was the National Soccer Coaches Association of America (NSCAA) State Technical Coordinator for Nebraska for five years, and holds a NSCAA Premier Diploma. He has been the head coach of the women's soccer program at Lincoln Lutheran High School in Lincoln, NE, since 2009. He writes a monthly article on coaching for the Star City Sports, Lincoln, NE.

Dave is currently Director of Environmental Studies, Director of Nebraska Earth Systems Education Network, Chair of Science for Educators, Masters of Applied Science, and Professor of Earth Science at the University of Nebraska–Lincoln. His professional work has been documented in more than 160 papers, reports, and abstracts. Dave serves as an elected member of the Executive

Committee of the Council of Environmental Deans and Directors (CEDD), which is part of the National Council for Science and the Environment (NCSE).

His current projects include the international, multi-institutional "Employing Model-Based Reasoning in Socio-Environmental Synthesis" (EMBeRS) working group, whose goal is to improve the ability of people to work on collaborative teams. He is on the management team for the InTeGrate project, a $10M NSF STEP grant. As part of this project, his role is to provide leadership and help educators integrate sustainability principles into science, technology, engineering, and mathematics (STEM) curriculums. Another component of his work has been to focus attention on the needs of students to be successful in the 21st-century workforce. He collaborates with Talent Training International on the application of their Trimetrix® assessment to students and players. Dave has been married for 31 years, and has two daughters who are pursuing their passions, one in physical therapy and one in religious life.

NOTES

INTRODUCTION

1.   http://www.ted.com/talks/drew_dudley_everyday_leaders hip/transcript?language=en.

CHAPTER 1. CHANGE YOUR FOCUS

2.   Bransford, J.D., Brown, A.L. and Cocking, R.E., eds. *How People Learn: Brain, Mind, Experience, and School: Expanded Sub Edition.* Committee on Developments in the Science of Learning with additional material from the Committee on Learning Research and Educational Practice and National Research Council (National Academies Press, 2000). ISBN: 978-0309070362.

CHAPTER 2. WHO ARE YOU AND WHY DOES IT MATTER?

3.   Conchie, Barry, and Hadd, Jerry. "Discovering How Your Future Leaders Think: The key questions your organization's coaches should ask every developing leader." *Gallup Management Journal,* November 10, 2005. http://www. gallup.com/businessjournal/19666/discovering-how-your-future-leaders-think.aspx.

4.   Johnson, Andy. *Pushing Back Entropy* (Restoration Publishing, 2014). ISBN: 978-0989339018.

5.   Gardner, Howard. *Frames of the Mind: The Theory of Multiple Intelligences,* 3rd ed. (New York: Basic Books, 2011). ISBN: 978-0465024339.

6.   Bonnstetter, B.J., and Suiter, J.I. *The Universal Language DISC Reference Manual,* 16th Printing (Target Training International, Ltd., 2013). ISBN: 978-0970753144. Marston, W.M. *Emotions of Normal People* (Harcourt, Brace, & Co., 1928). Reprinted: *Emotions of Normal People* (Talent Training International, Ltd., 2013) with Introduction by Bill Bonnstetter and Epilogue by Ron Bonnstetter. ISBN: 978-0970753168. Also: Marston, William Moulton. *Emotions of Normal People* (Cooper Press, 2014). ISBN: 978-1406701166.

7.   Sinek, Simon. *Start with Why: How Great Leaders Inspire Everyone to Take Action* (Portfolio, 2009). ISBN: 978-1591842804.

8.   Spranger, E. *Types of Men: The Psychology and Ethics of Personality* (New York: G.E. Stechert Co., 1928). Reprinted: *Types of Men* (Target Training International, Ltd., 2013) with Introduction by Bill Bonnstetter and Epilogue by Ron Bonnstetter. ISBN: 978-0970753137. [Original Work by Lebebsformen; Halle (Saale): Niemeyerm, 1914.]

9.   http://greenpeakpartners.com/resources/docs/GreenPeak Commentary.pdf; http://greenpeakpartners.com/resources/docs/6%2015%2010%20Chief%20Learning%20Officer.pdf; http://greenpeakpartners.com/resources/docs/7%2015%2010%20Human%20Resource%20Executive.pdf.

10. Bennis, W. *On Becoming a Leader,* 20th Anniversary Edition/3rd Edition (Basic Books, 2003). ISBN: 0738208175.

CHAPTER 3. WHO ARE YOU AND WHAT ARE YOUR PHILOSOPHIES, VALUES, AND ETHICS?

11. Beswick, B. *Focused for Soccer: Develop a Winning Mental Approach* (Human Kinetics, 2001). Second edition published by Human Kinetics, 2010. ISBN: 978-0736084116.

12. Ibid.

13. Lencioni, P. *The Five Dysfunctions of a Team: A Leadership Fable* (Jossey-Bass, 2002). ISBN: 978-0787960759.

CHAPTER 4. UNDERSTAND WHOM YOU ARE COACHING/LEADING/EDUCATING

14. Lencioni, P. *The Five Dysfunctions of a Team: A Leadership Fable* (Jossey-Bass, 2002). ISBN: 978-0787960759.

15. Bonnstetter, B.J., and Suiter, J.I. *The Universal Language DISC Reference Manual,* 16th Printing (Target Training International, Ltd., 2013). ISBN: 978-0970753144.

16. Ibid.

17. Piaget, J. *Success and Understanding* (Cambridge, MA: Harvard University Press, 1978). ISBN: 978-0674853874.

18. Marston, C. *Motivating the 'What's in It for Me' Workforce: Manage Across the Generational Divide and Increase Profits* (John Wiley and Sons, 2007).ISBN: 978-0470124147.

19. Howe, N., and Strauss, W. *Millennials Rising: The Next Great Generation* (Vintage Books. 2000). ISBN: 978-0375707193.

20. Dorrance, A. *Training Soccer Champions* (JTC Sports Inc., 1996). Reprinted with foreword by Tim Nash (Echo Point Books & Media, 2014). ISBN: 978-1626549203.

21. Helgeson, S., and Johnson, J. *The Female Vision: Women's Real Power at Work* (San Francisco, CA: Berrett-Koehler Publishers, Inc., (2010). ISBN: 978-1576753828.

22. Price, R., and Lisk, R. *The Complete Leader: Everything You Need to Become a High-Performing Leader* (Aloha Publishing, 2014). ISBN: 978-1612060835.

23. Gosselin, D., Cooper, S., Bonnstetter, R.J., and Bonnstetter, B. "Exploring the Assessment of 21st Century Professional Competencies of Undergraduate Students in Environmental Studies through a Business–Academic Partnership," *Journal of Environmental Studies and Science*, 2013, 3, 359–368. DOI 10.1007/s13412-013-0140-1.

24. Dweck, C.S. *Mindset: The New Psychology of Success* (Ballantine Books, 2006). ISBN: 978-0345472328.

CHAPTER 5. WHAT DOES THE END LOOK LIKE?

25. Wiggins, G., and McTighe, J. *Essential Questions: Opening Doors to Student Understanding* (Alexandria, VA: Association for Supervision and Curriculum Development (ASCD), 2013). ISBN: 978-1416615057.

26. Gosselin, D.C., Levy, R.H., and Bonnstetter R.J. "Utilizing Earth Science Research to Improve Understanding Between Scientists and Educators." *Journal of Geoscience Education*, 2003, 51 (1), 114-120.

27. Buckingham, M., and Coffman, C. *First, Break All the Rules: What the World's Greatest Managers Do Differently* (Simon & Schuster, 1999). ISBN: 978-0684852867.

CHAPTER 6. HOW NOT TO GET TO THE END-IN-MIND: START ASSUMING!

28. Beswick, B. *Focused for Soccer: Develop a Winning Mental Approach* (Human Kinetics, 2001). Second edition published by Human Kinetics, 2010. ISBN 978-0736084116.

CHAPTER 7. HOW TO GET TO THE END-IN-MIND: HOW PEOPLE LEARN + COLLABORATION

29. Zull, J.E. "The Art of Changing the Brain." *Teaching for Meaning* 2004, 62(1), 68-72.

30. Zull, J.E. *The Art of Changing the Brain: Enriching the Practice of Teaching by Exploring the Biology of Learning* (Stylus Publishing, LLC, 2002). ISBN: 978-1579220549.

31. Zull, J.E. "The Art of Changing the Brain." *Teaching for Meaning* 2004, 62(1), 68-72.

32. Ibid.

33. For example: Cobb, P. "Theories of Mathematical Learning and Constructivism: A Personal View." Paper presented at the *Symposium on Trends and Perspectives in Mathematics Education*, 1994, Institute for Mathematics, University of Klagenfurt, Austria. Piaget, J. *Success and Understanding* (Cambridge, MA: Harvard University Press, 1978). Vygotsky, L.S. *Mind in Society: The Development of Higher Psychological Processes*, 14th ed. (Cambridge: Harvard University Press, 1978).

34. Bransford, J.D., Brown, A.L., and Cocking, R.E., editors. *How People Learn: Brain, Mind, Experience, and School: Expanded Sub Edition.* Committee on Developments in the Science of Learning with additional material from the Committee on Learning Research and Educational Practice and National Research Council (National Academies Press, 2000). ISBN: 978-0309070362.

35. Brembs, B., Lorenzetti, F. D., Reys, F. D., Baxter, D. A., and Byrne, J. H. "Operant Reward Learning in Aplysia: Neuronal Correlates and Mechanisms." *Science*, 2002, 296(5573), 1706–1710.

36. Friend, M., and Cook, L. *Interactions: Collaboration Skills for School Professionals,* 2nd ed. (White Plains, NY: Longman, 1996). Newer 7th edition: (Pearson, 2012). ISBN: 978-0132774925.

37. Bybee, R., Taylor, J., et al. *The BSCS 5E Instructional Model: Origins and Effectiveness* (Colorado Springs, CO: BSCS, 2006). Newer edition: Bybee, Rodger. *The BSCS 5E Instructional Model - Creating Teachable Moments* (PB356X) (National Science Teachers Association - NSTA Press, 2015). ISBN: 978-1941316009.

38. Ibid.

CHAPTER 8. HOW DO YOU ASSESS SUCCESS?

39. Pink, D. H. *Drive: The Surprising Truth about What Motivates Us* (Penguin Books, LTD, 2009).

40. Ibid.

41. Dweck, C.S. *Mindset: The New Psychology of Success* (Ballantine Books, 2006). ISBN: 978-0345472328.

42. Thompson, J. *The Power of Double-Goal Coaching: Developing Winners in Sports and Life* (Balanced Sports Publishing, LLC, 2010). ISBN: 978-0982131749.

43. Gosselin, D.C., Thomas, J., Redmond, A., Larson-Miller, C., Cooper, S., Bonnstetter, R.J., and Slater, T.F. "Laboratory Earth: A Model of Online K-12 Teacher Coursework." *Journal of Geoscience Education*, 2010, 58(4) 203-213.

44. Livingston, J. A. "Metacognition: An Overview," 1997. Retrieved December 27, 2011, from http://gse.buffalo.edu/fas/shuell/CEP564/Metacog.htm.

45. For example: Bixler, B. A. "The effects of scaffolding students' problem-solving process via question prompts on

problem solving and intrinsic motivation in an online learning environment." 2008 PhD diss., The Pennsylvania State University, State College, PA. Chang, M. M. "Enhancing Web-based language learning through self-monitoring." *Journal of Computer Assisted Learning,* 2007, 23(3), 187–96. Chung, S., Chung., M.-J., and Severance, C. "Design of support tools and knowledge building in a virtual university course: Effect of reflection and self-explanation prompts." Paper presented at the *WebNet 99 World Conference on the WWW and Internet Proceedings,* October 1999, Honolulu, Hawaii. (ERIC Document Reproduction Service No. ED448706). Crippen, K. J., and Earl, B.L. "The impact of Web-based worked examples and self-explanation on performance, problem solving, and self-efficacy." *Computers & Education,* 2007 49(3), 809–21.

46. Kaplan, R. S. and Norton, D. P. "Putting the Balanced Scorecard to Work." *Harvard Business Review,* 1993.

47. Ibid.

48. Lewis, R. W. *Measuring, Reporting and Appraising Results of Operations with Reference to Goals, Plans and Budgets, Planning, Managing and Measuring the Business: A Case Study of Management Planning and Control at General Electric Company* (New York: Controllership Foundation, 1955).

CHAPTER 9. COMMUNICATION: THE FOUNDATION FOR CHANGING MINDSETS

49. Lencioni, P. *The Five Dysfunctions of a Team: A Leadership Fable* (Jossey-Bass, 2002). ISBN: 978-0787960759.

50. http://howwelead.org/2015/01/07/feedback-is-the-breakfast -of-champions-2/.

51. Pink, D. H. *Drive: The Surprising Truth about What Motivates Us* (Penguin Books, LTD, 2009).

52.   Mehrabian, Albert. *Silent Messages: Implicit Communication of Emotions and Attitudes* (Wadsworth Publishing Company, 1972). ISBN: 978-0534000592.

53.   Medina, John. *Brain Rules (Updated and Expanded): 12 Principles for Surviving and Thriving at Work, Home, and School*, 2nd ed. (Pear Press, 2014). ISBN: 978-0983263371.

54.   Kimmel, M.S. *The Gendered Society* (New York, NY: Oxford University Press, 2000). Newer, 5th ed.: Oxford University Press, 2012. ISBN: 978-0199927463.

55.   Lott, B. *Women's Lives: Themes and Variations in Gender Learning* (Monterey, CA: Brooks/Cole, 1987). ISBN: 978-0534074401.

56.   Dorrance, A. *Training Soccer Champions* (JTC Sports Inc., 1996). Reprinted with foreword by Tim Nash (Echo Point Books & Media, 2014). ISBN: 978-1626549203.

57.   Ibid.

58.   Silby, C., and Smith, S. *Games Girls Play: Understanding and Guiding Female Athletes* (New York, NY: St. Martin's Press, 2000). ISBN: 978-0312261634.

CHAPTER 10. BRING IT ALL TOGETHER: TAKE ON NEW CHALLENGES

59.   Lencioni, P. *The Five Dysfunctions of a Team: A Leadership Fable* (Jossey-Bass, 2002). ISBN: 978-0787960759.